CHRISTINA STEAD

Univ Nott

KEY
WOMEN
WRITERS
EDITOR: SUE ROE

CHRISTINA STEAD

SUSAN SHERIDAN

Lecturer in Women's Studies
The Flinders University of South Australia

NOTTINGHAM UNIVERSITY LIBRARY

HARVESTER · WHEATSHEAF

NEW YORK   LONDON   TORONTO   SYDNEY   TOKYO

First published 1988 by
Harvester Wheatsheaf
66 Wood Lane End,
Hemel Hempstead, Hertfordshire, HP2 4RG

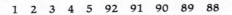

A division of
Simon & Schuster International Group

© 1988, Susan Sheridan

All rights reserved. No part of this publication may
be reproduced, stored in a retrieval system, or
transmitted, in any form, or by any means,
electronic, mechanical, photocopying, recording or
otherwise, without the prior permission, in writing,
from the publisher.

Printed and bound in Great Britain by
Billing and Sons Ltd., Worcester

British Library Cataloguing in Publication Data

Sheridan, Susan, 1944–
Christina Stead.—(Key women writers).
1. Fiction in English. Australian writer.
Stead, Christina, 1901–1983. Critical
studies
I. Title   II. Series
823

ISBN 0-7108-0998-0
ISBN 0-7108-1072-5 Pbk

1 2 3 4 5 92 91 90 89 88

331153

In memory of my mother

Titles in the Key Women Writers Series

Gillian Beer	*George Eliot*
Paula Bennett	*Emily Dickinson*
Penny Boumelha	*Charlotte Brontë*
Stevie Davies	*Emily Brontë*
Kate Fullbrook	*Katherine Mansfield*
Anne Green	*Madame de Lafayette*
Deborah Johnson	*Iris Murdoch*
Angela Leighton	*Elizabeth Barrett Browning*
Jane Marcus	*Rebecca West*
Rachel Blau DuPlessis	*H.D.*
Jean Radford	*Dorothy Richardson*
Lorna Sage	*Angela Carter*
Susan Sheridan	*Christina Stead*
Patsy Stoneman	*Elizabeth Gaskell*
Nicole Ward Jouve	*Colette*
Jane Heath	*Simone de Beauvoir*
Rebecca Ferguson	*Alice Walker*
Coral Ann Howells	*Jean Rhys*
Kate Flint	*Virginia Woolf*

Key Women Writers
Series Editor: Sue Roe

The *Key Women Writers* series has developed in a spirit of challenge, exploration and interrogation. Looking again at the work of women writers with established places in the mainstream of the literary tradition, the series asks, in what ways can such writers be regarded as feminist? Does their status as canonical writers ignore the notion that there are ways of writing and thinking which are specific to women? Or is it the case that such writers have integrated within their writing a feminist perspective which so subtly maintains its place that these are writers who have, hitherto, been largely misread?

In answering these questions, each volume in the series is attentive to aspects of composition such as style and voice, as well as to the ideas and issues to emerge out of women's writing practice. For while recent developments in literary and feminist theory have played a significant part in the creation of the series, feminist theory represents no specific methodology, but rather an opportunity to broaden our range of responses to the issues of history, psychology and gender which have always engaged women writers. A new and creative dynamics between a woman critic and her female subject has been made possible by recent developments in feminist theory, and the series seeks to reflect the important critical insights which have emerged out of this new, essentially feminist, style of engagement.

It is not always the case that literary theory can be directly transposed from its sources in other disciplines to the practice of reading writing by women. The series investigates the possibility that a distinction may need to be made between feminist politics and the literary criticism of women's writing which has not, up to now, been sufficiently emphasized. Feminist reading, as well as feminist writing, still needs to be constantly interpreted and re-interpreted. The complexity and range of choices implicit in this procedure are represented throughout the series. As works of criticism, all the volumes in the series represent wide-ranging and creative styles of discourse, seeking at all times to express the particular resonances and perspectives of individual women writers.

Sue Roe

Contents

Preface

Christina Stead is a controversial figure. Her reputation as a 'key writer', a major figure in twentieth-century literature, has not yet been firmly enough established to elicit the usual bibliographical and biographical appurtenances of mainstream recognition.[1] It has fluctuated between fame and obscurity, from the time her first books appeared in 1934 and she was hailed as a major new talent until the years before her death in 1983 when there was talk of a nomination for the Nobel Prize, and she received several prestigious awards and honours.

Over the past half-century different groups have emphasized different aspects of her work: Australians have read her as an expatriate writer, many critics have noted her closeness to European rather than English literary traditions, some US writers have praised her as a major figure in their generation, leftists claim her because of her well-known but scantily documented political affiliations, and the fact that her main publisher in recent years has been the British feminist press, Virago, indicates the widespread interest in her as a woman writer. This book sets out to address many of the issues raised by linking Stead's fiction with feminism. In doing so, it participates in the wider debate which rages around her literary reputation.

To explain the phenomenon of her unstable reputation as a major writer, one would need to take into account this variety of claims on her name, and her marginal location relative to all three Anglophone literatures with which she is associated. Then there is, inevitably, the matter of her writing's distinctiveness, which refuses neat accommodation into any of the usual regional, generic or stylistic categories of modern fiction. Moreover, a writer of the Left whose main period of productivity coincides with the Second World War and the Cold War is hardly well placed to achieve due recognition. There are also factors such as her dislike of literary professionalism in general and of self-promotion in particular, and the unexplained gap in her publishing record between 1952 and 1966. Her wandering life and the vagaries of her publishing history seem, however, to be the major factors contributing to the relative obscurity of this major writer.

Born in Sydney in 1902, where she died in 1983, Christina Stead spent most of her writing life in England, Europe and the United States. Arriving in London in 1928, she met the man who was to be her life partner, the United States writer, Marxist and merchant banker, William Blake, and until his death in 1968 they travelled widely, spending much of the 1930s in Paris, the war years in New York and Hollywood, several years after that moving around various European cities, and the period after 1952 in London. Between 1934 and 1952 nine of her fifteen books appeared, in most cases with both London and New York publishers. These included the three most often regarded as her major achievements: *House of All Nations* (1938), *The Man Who Loved Children* (1940) and *For Love Alone* (1944). From 1952 to 1965 she published no books of her own, only two translations from French. Then, after this long silence, reprints of four earlier books appeared over 1965–66 in New York and Sydney, she published a major new novel under different titles in New York (*Dark Places of the Heart* in 1966) and London (*Cotters' England* in 1967), and the collection of novellas, *The Puzzleheaded Girl* (1967).

At this time some major US writers paid tribute to Stead's work: Randall Jarrell in his Introduction to the reprint of *The Man Who Loved Children*, Susan Sontag, Elizabeth Hardwick, Saul Bellow.[2] Renewed Australian attention was expressed in the first book-length study of her work, by R.G. Geering (1969), and in several reprints from publishers Angus and Robertson. After her return to Australia in 1975, two more novels appeared: *The Little Hotel* (1975) and *Miss Herbert* (1976). Both of these, like *Cotters' England*, had been substantially written in the early 1950s, and this was also the case with the posthumously published *I'm Dying Laughing* (1987). Her literary executor, R.G. Geering, edited this long-awaited 'Hollywood novel' for publication, and also the collection of short pieces, *Ocean of Story* (1985).

The picture that emerges from this sketch is a discontinuous writing and publishing career, together with a broken pattern of publication with different houses. Margaret Harris's forthcoming study of the conditions of publication and reception of Christina Stead's work will fill out the details, but it is possible at this stage to speculate that these discontinuities and the subsequent unavailability of her books contributed to the lack of steady recognition that her fiction has suffered. Another factor here is undoubtedly that of demand: without a wide popular audience, her books could still have kept in circulation had there been strong academic interest, but this was not forthcoming. Despite the enthusiasm of other writers and of younger critics in the late 1960s, by 1977 at the Modern Languages Association conference in Chicago, a session devoted to Christina Stead's work attracted only seven or eight participants, all of them, like myself, young women interested in feminism.[3]

Christina Stead

However in Australia, since the long-overdue introduction of courses on Australian literature in the universities in the 1960s, there has been a steady interest in her work, especially in her two novels with local settings, *Seven Poor Men of Sydney* (1934) and *For Love Alone* (1944), and in the autobiographically-based *The Man Who Loved Children* (1940). Something of a prodigal returned, Stead was much sought after by interviewers and became popularly known in Australia during the last years of her life.[4] Her reputation among critics tends to fluctuate between the emphasis on her 'Australianness' and the claim that her work manifests 'universal' values.

A major reason for the present upsurge of interest in Christina Stead, however, is the interest in women writers associated with feminism. Yet her reputation in this context is hotly contested by 'malestream' literary critics who have attacked feminists for 'enlisting her work in support of partisan causes' and misreading her texts by an over-emphasis on certain features such as her 'ruthless portraits of male egotism' or the 'reductive labelling' of her female characters as feminist heroines.[5] Ironically, this attack acquired additional ammunition from Christina Stead herself, who disclaimed any particular interest in the position of women and any respect for feminism as a political movement. Nevertheless, the Virago reprints series *has* placed her work in a feminist context (loosely defined), at the same time as it has made her work widely available throughout the Anglophone world. Inevitably, perhaps, it has also tended to play down the Australian contexts of her work. As an Australian as well as a feminist, I might be said, by those who maintain that a universal and objective critical stance is possible and desirable, to run a double risk of partisanship in my approach.[6] But since feminist criticism holds no such belief, it might rather be said that I have a doubly intense involvement in the debate, a double advantage. My relationship as feminist critic with my subject is of necessity combative but I hope it will prove also to be 'a new and creative dynamic', as the general editor of this series puts it.

To discuss Stead's writing by focusing on its possible relations with feminist theory and criticism, is, then, to intervene in a hotly contested debate. At stake in this debate are both her reputation as a key writer, a literary 'proper name', and also the status of feminist readings of her as a woman writer. The feminist approach I offer here places Stead's continuing fascination with women's lives in tension with her rejection of feminism. I have chosen to analyse a selection of her novels, those with female protagonists, as powerful fictional explorations of women and gender relations in modern culture—as 'lives of modern women'. At the same time, the selection of her novels read in this way throws into question some of the dominant strategies of feminist literary studies and some of the dominant assumptions of feminist theory generally. The result demonstrates, I believe, that fiction can productively question theory as well as vice versa. In the chapters which follow, I have attempted to set up a dialogue between some of her novels and contemporary feminist theories of literary production and of gendered subjectivity as it is historically produced in culture: to re-read both kinds of text in relation to one another.

Acknowledgements

I am indebted to the Humanities Research Centre at the Australian National University for the Visiting Fellowship in 1986 which enabled me to begin writing this book, and to Deakin University for generously granting me leave to take it up. The Flinders University of South Australia, and in particular my colleague in the Women's Studies Unit, Lyndall Ryan, have made it possible for me to complete the book during my first year of appointment here, and for that I am very grateful. At the National Library of Australia, Ms Pam Ray and her staff in the Manuscripts Room, where I was able to consult the Christina Stead papers, were most helpful. Like all Stead readers and scholars, I owe a debt of gratitude to her literary executor, Professor R.G. Geering, for making these papers available and for the posthumous publications he has edited, and I thank him for permission to quote from the manuscript material.

Since the time in 1973 when I was a postgraduate student at Adelaide University and Ian Reid introduced me to Stead's fiction, I have discussed ideas about it with so many colleagues, students and friends that the list of those I ought to acknowledge would be too long to print, even if I could compile it accurately. I fear that the same is true of those whose writing—on Stead, or in the field of feminist criticism—has influenced me. I have tried to acknowledge as many of these as possible in the notes to

Acknowledgements

my text which is, like all writing, itself a tissue of quotations. In particular, though, I am grateful for discussions about Christina Stead, feminism and writing with Angela Carter, Anna Gibbs, Sneja Gunew, Margaret Harris, Drusilla Modjeska, Meaghan Morris and Jenny Pausacker, and I thank Sneja Gunew especially for her initial support and continuing encouragement of this project. My heartfelt thanks go to Susan Magarey, who has been involved throughout the planning and writing of this book, refusing to countenance my moments of despair about it, and who read the whole typescript through critically and constructively. Any obscurities or inelegancies of phrasing that remain are my responsibility entirely, as are any lapses in accuracy or argument. Finally, I want to acknowledge the women of the feminist movement, without whom this book would have been impossible.

The author and publisher would like to thank the following for permission to reproduce copyright material: Professor R.G. Geering and the estate of Christina Stead; Lawrence Pollinger Limited, Joan Daves, Angus & Robertson and Penguin Australia for quotations from the novels and stories of Christina Stead.

Chapter One

Writer and Reader: Critical Issues

The Writer and Feminism

'Oh, I would hate it! I'd hate it!' was Christina Stead's reply when asked in an interview whether she would like to identify with the Women's Liberation movement.[1] In this and other interviews she reiterated the opinion that it was not a genuinely political movement, but middle-class, fanatical, 'pure freakery'. She maintained that women were no more oppressed than men by economic and social restrictions on their freedom, although they were still sexually suppressed in relation to men; that the problems for women in getting 'equal pay for equal work, and crêches, and liberation from domestic drudgery' were like union matters which required no autonomous women's movement; and that separatist strategies of women's living and working collectives were 'disgraceful and disorderly' in that they denied connection with men who are, she declared, 'women's natural friends and companions'. She spoke of the movement as being led by 'political types' who cared nothing for ordinary women, whom she characterized as 'the poor little struggling housewife'.[2]

This vehement rejection of feminism did not coincide with a belief that literature is beyond politics. Stead was always happy to agree that she was a writer of the Left, that her view of things was informed by Marxism as well as by an early interest in revolutionary history and in the Australian tradition of political radicalism,[3] although she was also adamant (survivor of the Cold War as she was) that broadcasting political messages was not the role of fiction. It seems that for her, feminism did not rate as a serious political engagement, neither a mode of analysis like Marxism nor a tradition of political activism like socialism. Her objections may shed light on her political formation during the period of backlash against feminism between the two world wars, and also on the discourses on women, gender difference, desire and power with which her fictional texts engage.

Among her unpublished papers there are several notes which suggest that she saw feminism as a dead issue, belonging to the suffragist past and in no need of revival. She refers to some older women activists whom she met in London on her arrival there in the late 1920s as 'veterans of old battles, faint echoes and tatters of buried issues'.[4] There is a note of admiration for the battlers here, but she would have nothing to do with feminist strategies of analysis or action. She comments with irritation on the 'endless tiresome mean comparisons between the fate of men and women' in Virginia Woolf's *A Room of One's Own* and asks, *a propos* of *Three Guineas*: 'What was the reason for Virginia's strange archaic outburst about women's rights in the hungering thirties?'.[5] It is striking how her comment, while insisting on the economic context, overlooks the *political* context written into Woolf's essay, the rise of fascism in England and Europe. Yet Stead's belief that there should no longer be any need for 'women's issues' once we had won the vote and access to positions in the public world was a common one, and indeed one that Woolf herself had shared, along with many others of that generation. For socialists and liberals alike, emancipation consisted in women's entry into the public world, in being no longer exclusively confined to the domestic realm, whether as wives, daughters or servants. For socialists, however, the public world was where history is made through the dynamic of class struggle, and women were to participate in this struggle through their unions or by supporting their worker husbands—not in distinct struggles undertaken on their own account, as women. An Australian who was at that time a member of the Communist Party has written:

> Thirty years ago we saw the struggle for women's emancipation as a minor part of a much larger struggle and equated their liberation with their entry into the work-force, socialization of housework and provision of child-care services. The solution of women's problems lay in lifting women, as far as their disabilities and biological role allowed, to the level of men.[6]

With an understanding of the dynamics of social change drawn from the Australian radical egalitarian tradition of which she became aware as a child and from the militant socialism of the European and North American intellectuals with whom she mixed during the 'hungering thirties', it is hardly surprising that Stead should react with impatience to the idea of another women's movement in the 1970s. So, too, did Doris Lessing in the 1972 Preface to *The Golden Notebook*, where she maintained that Women's Liberation was already out of date in 'the cataclysms we are living through'.[7] That Stead should automatically label it 'middle-class' and out of touch with 'poor housewives' echoes Old Left suspicions of the earlier women's movement as a struggle limited to equal rights liberalism.

3

Yet she would speak of women's writing as a culturally and historically determined phenomenon in a way that is basic to any feminist analysis of women's position as cultural producers:

> No doubt because I was brought up by a naturalist, I have always felt an irresistible urge to paint true pictures of society as I have seen it. I often felt that quite well known writings lacked truth, and this was particularly so of the pictures of women, I felt, not only because women took their complete part in society but were not represented as doing so, but because the long literary tradition, thousands of years old, had enabled men completely to express themselves, while women feared to do so. However, my object was by no means to write for women, or to discuss feminine problems, but to depict society as it was.... Naturally, I wished to understand men and women equally.[8]

This statement, one of her more expansive comments on the subject of women and writing, pre-dates the current feminist movement and lacks the defensive note that marks her later interviews on the subject. Yet it is typical in its emphasis on the role of the writer as a truth-teller of a particular kind: the specification of point of view ('as I saw it') together with her self-description as a naturalist, trained by her scientist father. Both an aesthetic and a philosophical naturalism are simultaneously suggested: 'naturally', she would be concerned with both men and women, 'society'; she often insisted that the 'natural' rightness of relations between the sexes was what feminists most destructively denied. At the same time, she feels a more urgent need to depict *women* truthfully because of the tradition of past misrepresentations, and acknowledges a disadvantage for women writers in attempting to express themselves in the context of such a tradition. The potential tension

4

between these two imperatives—to redress the balance of representations of women, but to range freely over 'society as it was', 'to understand men and women equally'—is apparently the source of her ambivalence about naming herself as a *woman* writer—an ambivalence shared, it should be said, by many others of her generation. And it is no doubt the spectre of being relegated to the devalued realms of 'women's writing' that lies behind her denial that she writes 'for women' or 'about feminine problems'.

Her comment on women's timidity, that they have feared to express themselves fully, is one that recurs in later interviews. Stead did praise the women's movement for encouraging women to write, to overcome their timidity and to compete in this arena with men.[9] Yet, while there is no question of women's being somehow inherently disadvantaged when it comes to writing, she implies that it is *only* this culturally-imposed timidity which has held women back. Her assumption, too, that to write is automatically to compete with men suggests how strongly the demarcation line between 'women's fiction' and serious literature is usually drawn, and how important it was to her to be considered a serious writer. A feminist would go on to ask why 'literature' is largely a male preserve and why women's timidity might be particularly noticeable in this arena.

These were the sorts of question which Stead declared herself unwilling to pursue, because she held a firm conviction that the public world of politics and culture was beyond gender difference. It was the realm of class struggle and the making of history and when women entered it, they did so as the comrades and equals of men. In the romantic eyes of Teresa, in *For Love Alone*, 'it was from the womb of time that she was fighting her way and the first day lay before her':

And suddenly as a strange thought it came to her, that she had reached the gates of the world of Girton and Quick and that it was towards them she was only now journeying, and in a direction unguessed by them; . . . and with her she felt many thousands of shadows, pressing along with her, storming forwards, but quietly and eagerly, though blindly.[10]

It is a vision sharply separated from the traditional world of 'the woman in the home', whom Stead described as 'often moneyless, powerless, often anxious, disturbed, wretched, with no status to speak of, no trades-union',[11] whom she had portrayed unforgettably in Henny, the wife of 'the man who loved children'. The metaphor for woman's entry into history, 'out of the womb of time' suggests that she leaves behind not only her infancy as a human being but also what Hegel called the 'nether world of women', of domesticity and the life of the body.[12]

In contrast, Virginia Woolf saw that world as an inheritance not to be left behind, even though it was burdensome. She articulated women's dilemma vividly when writing of George Eliot's traversal of the two spheres:

The burden and complexity of womanhood were not enough; she must reach beyond the sanctuary and pluck for herself the strange bright fruits of art and knowledge. Clasping them as few women have ever clasped them, she would not renounce her own inheritance—the difference of view, the difference of standard. . . .[13]

In Stead's fiction the feminine 'difference of standard' does not translate into the terms of the male-dominated world of culture and politics. She represents women's entry into the public world as an historical phenomenon accompanied by enormous confusions as they attempt to find their own way in new territory. For Teresa: 'Here where she stood no old wives' tale and no mother's sad sneer, no father's admonition, reached'; her feminine inheritance seems to have no bearing on 'this rough and tumble of need, egotism and love' among men, yet she has travelled there on a different route from the men.[14] Women's difference, for Stead, is not a socially experienced position from which a woman must negotiate her relation to the public world, because she conceived of the public world as universal, gender-neutral.

Such a conception confirms Stead's dismissal of feminism as a valid political position and should, logically, render feminist readings of her texts impossible. But perhaps, here, logic is too simple. The vehemence of her dismissal is in excess of this logic. The key terms in her condemnation of feminism, terms that are reiterated in the interviews we began with, are: the 'natural' bond between women and men, the 'disgraceful and disorderly' upsetting of that natural bond by women's bonding with each other, and the protectiveness implied by her adjectives for the 'poor little struggling housewives' supposedly ignored by the movement. These terms come together in an astonishing homophobic outburst published in *Partisan Review* in 1979, in response to a questionnaire:

Lesbians sometimes wish to better women's lot and they may do so, as any other women; but their inclination often is to separate women from men and discourage women's natural affection for men; they play upon the greatest weakness of women, their cultivated timidity, and rob them of one of the best and most momentous things in life, love of a man. Lesbians fighting for their own interests are no more suited to the women's movement than so-called gay liberation is suited to the trades union movement; it is quite out of context.[15]

In this text the feminist movement is accepted as a kind of trades union for women, and the problem is relocated as 'lesbians' (categorically distinguished from 'women') who have no place there. The lesbian is characterized as a predator from whom 'women' need protection. The normative implications of heterosexual desire being designated always as 'natural' emerge as a kind of sexual essentialism which might seem to contradict Stead's expressed belief in the cultural constructedness of femininity ('cultivated timidity', for instance). Yet the two tendencies are set up in a workable opposition in the sentence which places heterosexual love as a superlative strength ('one of the best and most momentous things in life') against a superlative weakness, namely 'the greatest weakness of women', their timidity. The rhetorical structure of opposition works to suggest, I think, that heterosexual love is necessary to women's freedom—that it is freedom *from* her femininity, her 'weakness', that a woman needs and will gain through a man's love. The desire of an 'unnatural' woman, a lesbian, would compound that weakness or, rather, exploit it in others.

What emerges from this reading of the passage is an underlying distrust of femininity for its weakness and susceptibility, and at the same time a strong animus against those women who reject the only 'solution' to feminine weakness, the love of a man. While Stead's fiction contains some of the most powerful representations of female desire to be found, that desire is usually seen as chaotic, 'disorderly' or decadent unless it is directed towards union with a man. Yet she remains preoccupied with female characters and their destinies, and her most memorable women are those in search of love, the social rebels and outlaws—'disorderly' women, in fact. Those who attempt to play by the rules, like Letty Fox and Eleanor Herbert, become objects of satire. The 'natural outlawry of womankind'[16] is a recurrent theme, though it is not romanticized: Stead is as interested in the destructive as the creative potential of those powers traditionally attributed to women:

> Women have benefited and suffered from this, which is related to the sex tabus and mysteries, to the white goddesses, to the wicked hag and the gingerbread house, 'the noonday witch', Goethe's 'eternal feminine'...to mariolatry, matriolatry and the lover's dream....Behind the concept of woman's strangeness is the idea that a woman may do anything: she is below society, not bound by its law, unpredictable; an attribute given to every member of the league of the unfortunate.[17]

But, she adds, their mythical function does not mean that such powers do not exist, for 'the slave, the woman, the dark-skinned alien' *do* have a different angle of vision: 'it is from underneath, for one thing; not to mention other differences, national, local, personal'.[18] It is characteristic of Stead to bring together the social and the mythic attributes of persons and to grant them both a reality. There could be, then, a female angle of vision, even although she did not set out 'to write for women, or to discuss feminine problems'.

A Challenge to Feminist Criticism

Many of Stead's stories of women's lives seem at first to invite the attention of feminist critics seeking in women's writing testimony to the common features of female experience which are not represented in patriarchal discourses. This feminism assumes that women's own words will grant unmediated access to the authenticity of their experience, and it gives priority to genres such as memoirs, journals, lyric poetry and autobiographical fiction. The search for women's accounts of female experience took on particular urgency in the context of early Women's Liberation sociological theories of sex-role conditioning, which often sounded so determinist in their account of how (as de Beauvoir put it) one is not born a woman but becomes one, that it was difficult to imagine women achieving any kind of authentic existence (her terminology).[19] This meant that the search for women's testimony often took on the additional object of finding 'positive images' of women, of those who rebelled against the cultural dicta that they remain silent and invisible and did so without paying the price of madness or death. As a consequence, the dominant approach in feminist literary criticism to date is geared to an autobiographical model of interpretation, to a revisionist quest for the buried tradition of feminist protest and to a thematics of sexual politics without a poetics of textual sexual politics.[20]

Stead's fiction may seem to invite this kind of critical approach, but seldom confirms its expectations about women's writing. Indeed, her novels can be read as a challenge to those particular feminist assumptions. First, while Stead claimed that all her characters were based on actual (auto)biographical models, her fictional modes—ranging from epic to satire and then the grotesque—produce characters that resist interpretation as models in the exemplary sense. Even the heroic characters in the novels based on her own life, Louisa and Teresa, are difficult to include among the ranks of models of female autonomy, in that one plans murder as her escape from the patriarchal family, while the other insists that her quest in life is 'for love alone'. Protagonists who devote themselves to culturally approved femininity are satirized, but Nellie in *Cotters' England*, the rebel who loudly and often proclaims her love for poor downtrodden women, is portrayed as positively evil. Second, then, the placing of Stead's characters in a tradition of 'feminist protest' is not appropriate.

With this model of feminist criticism, the feminism that is its object is sought in the text—or even in the writer herself—as a recognizable angry or subversive protest against the oppression of women. Stead's texts resist this approach and challenge its assumptions. To offer an alternative feminist reading, then, we need to locate feminism in the reading process, rather than in the text; to offer readings from feminist positions rather than seeking to uncover a feminism already present in the text. This involves a 'strong' concept of reading as the appropriation of a text to produce meaning: to read, in Barthes' words, is to 'produce the text, open it out, set it going'.[21] For feminist criticism, it means giving up the claim that we are rediscovering a pre-existent (feminist) vision of the author's, and acknowledging that as critics we begin from various pre-textual (feminist) positions which shape the questions that are brought into productive relation with the text. It means, too, arguing that all readings are political, in the sense that they are pre-textually positioned in ideology and belong to a particular historical discursive formation: all readings, and not only feminist ones, are appropriations of the text.[22]

A feminist criticism angled in this way need not confine itself to women's writing nor even to texts which address or construct female subjects, but it may have a particular interest in such texts' transformations of sexual and textual norms. To read Stead's fictions of modern women from such a position is to read not for 'images of women' in the exemplary sense nor for authentic testimonials of female experience, but rather to highlight, in the texts of a writer centrally concerned with what she called 'the psychological drama of the

11

person', the work of discursive constructions of femininity in fiction. This feminist reading, keeping an eye on its own textual relations, wants therefore to attend not only to representations of woman, or the thematics of sexual politics, but also to the text's positioning of the reader in language, or its sexual/textual poetics. It is a feminist discourse which politicizes the term 'woman'— and also the terms 'man', 'humanity', and so on. Within the discursive space made by this 'textual' feminism we can talk about 'the woman writer' or 'the woman reader' without collapsing 'woman' into a traditionally patriarchal essentialism.[23]

Stead's texts offer an especially vivid demonstration of the work of ideology in language, in discourses. There is little description and documentation, even less narratorial comment: the characters speak themselves and their world into textual existence, as it were. Dramatic monologues, spoken or 'thought'—'great arias and recitatives of self-deceit, self-justification, attempted manipulation'[24]—constitute the bulk of the novels, which are in general loosely structured in a series of scenes. The foregrounding of linguistic processes achieved by this structuring technique demonstrates the incessant inscription of ideologies in fantasy and dreams as well as rationally formulated ideas. The ideological structures and textures of mental life, with its fluid relations between the conscious and the unconscious, are the material of Stead's fiction.[25]

Men as well as women are constructed in this way, as the writing presents the surfaces of their lives as the real, refusing the temptation to promise some essential truth behind the masks of gender. Stead's salutary refusal to idealize some essential woman beneath the melodrama and the clichés of contemporary femininity in these constructions is particularly notable, for it proposes, contrary to some feminist accounts of gendered subjectivity, that we *are* what we act, that femininity is lived as it is performed in society and culture. The narrative enacts splits between these patriarchal ideologies and women's desires, yet both are presented as equally part of their reality, and not, as in liberal humanism, as the shadow and the substance of experience. As we observed in Stead's comments on the powers traditionally attributed to women, the apparently 'natural' sexual and aggressive desires which erupt to wreak havoc within the social order can be seen as themselves constructed by their very exclusion from that order's definition of femininity.

The concept of the linguistic construction of subjectivity may also be addressed by way of Stead's interesting comments on melodrama as a given set of 'regulation remarks just like a play' that people fall back upon in a crisis, [26] which is 'a relief, it is cut and dried for them'.[27] But what she suggests here as an explanation of certain linguistic behaviour is made to work beyond the 'cut and dried' in her fiction. Her melodramatic crisis scenes are usually family fights, like the brilliant opening sequence of *For Love Alone*, where 'regulation remarks' are so placed as to call up the whole cultural scenario of patriarchal relations between father and daughter. Teresa, goaded by the sexual teasing of 'the handsome man, the family god' bursts out, 'I will kill you, father', words which hang in the air as she rages on through the repertoire of rebellion to the accusation: '"When we are all suffering so much," she cried through her hair and folded arms, "you torture us" '; but the next line, while representing the restoration of the father's authority, also draws ironic attention to the daughters' domestic service in the family: ' "Meanwhile," said the beautiful man quietly, "you are letting Kitty do all the work".'[28] The 'regulation remarks', both melodramatic and domestic-banal, reverberate with their inter-textual associations ranging from Cinderella to Antigone to Hollywood movies.

In this scene, as in many others, 'heightened and polarized words and gestures' dramatize 'primary psychic roles, father, mother, child, and express basic psychic conditions'. Characterizing Balzac's melodramatic imagination in this way, Peter Brooks goes on to point out that 'the metaphoric texture of the prose itself suggests polarization into moral absolutes'.[29] At this point, Stead's prose no longer bears comparison with that of her admired Balzac, for it is precisely its *lack* of moral colouring which often unsettles and disorients readers. But this is crucial to her technique of having characters present themselves, in their own words. It is also crucial to her conception of the self or the inner life as a space defined by the formative discourses of a particular social place and time. It is not conceived of in the manner of liberal humanism as the realm of moral agency, and what potential freedom it has is often only achieved 'against the very grain of what we take to be human feeling'. Pointing this out, Angela Carter goes on:

> if her novels are read as novels about our lives, rather than about the circumstances that shape our lives, they are bound to disappoint, because the naturalist or high-bourgeois mode works within the convention that there is such a thing as 'private life'.[30]

The Interview and the Life of the Author

The tendency to read her as a naturalist writer has been reinforced by Stead herself, who always responded to questions about narrative moral and political judgements by declaring that she was a 'naturalist', like her father before her, and would no more condemn certain kinds of

14

behaviour than she would 'criticize a dingo for being a dingo'.[31] (It is interesting that she chose a predatory creature to illustrate this point, for she would often in the same interviews describe her relation to her protagonists—or, rather, to their actual models—as something like an obsession, 'like falling in love, or a stone hitting you'[32].) But her claim to truthfulness of observation the naturalist's model was not necessarily a claim to 'objectivity', and her narrative stance suggests that she shared the view that she attributes to Letty Fox, that 'Mere observation is not enough. The examiner must take part.... Sympathy and antipathy are two instruments of observation.'[33]

It is time to ask some questions about the status of such authorial statements, for they have been influential in shaping the way her work has been read and also in producing interdictions on certain readings, feminist ones in particular. At the time of her death in 1983 there were probably as many interviews with Stead in circulation as there were articles discussing her work. Her generosity in giving interviews is matched only by an apparent willingness to reveal the secrets of her novels in ways that modern writers almost never do: 'It's no secret he's (Sam Pollit) a portrait of my father';[34] 'Well, of course she didn't try to poison her stepmother but she thought about it';[35] and many similar comments about the prototypes of her characters such as 'You can't invent people, or they're puppets.'[36] These claims about her characters being irreducibly actual dovetail neatly with the claims about her naturalist's method. Both kinds of statement, and anecdotes to illustrate them, are repeated in every interview. In insisting on fact and observation, they refuse to authorize interpretation of any kind, but especially generalizations about what cultural phenomena might be represented in her fiction.

Just as she would not agree to describing *House of All*

Nations as a critique of capitalist high finance, so she would not agree that the family of *The Man Who Loved Children* was representative of the modern patriarchal nuclear family. Individual psychology, she implied, would explain her characters and their conflicts, and she insisted that the family be seen as normal, merely an incompatible combination of persons—Sam not a monster, Henny not a victim, the children not martyrs. 'Normal' is a term of approbation she used in conjunction with the psychological theory she favoured over psychoanalysis: 'Freud is really for the abnormal, the unbalanced, but because of his lovely sexual line he was taken over by everybody.'[37]

What emerges from the interviews is a cluster of self-descriptions which project an authorial persona in clear strong outlines: one for whom 'interpretation' is beside the point and for whom 'talking about writing has nothing to do with writing'.[38] It is a persona apparently resistant to most critical purposes except the biographical, and indeed it is employed in critical commentaries in much the way that autobiographical writings are used, as offering privileged access to the author, the originating subject of the fiction.

In particular, the authorial persona effectively sets up and legitimates an autobiographical reading of her two best-known novels, *The Man Who Loved Children* and *For Love Alone*, a reading which is limiting but authoritative and has been preferred by most critics, feminist and non-feminist alike. The autobiographical continuities between the two novels are taken to justify reading them together as a single *Bildungsroman* which, like *Sons and Lovers*, explores the social and psychological dynamics of the author's formation in the family. Indeed, their similarities come to be seen as more significant than their differences of setting and treatment. As well, they are read more as documents than as fictions: Dorothy

Green describes the two novels, together with *Seven Poor Men of Sydney*, as 'one of the most remarkable accounts ever written of what it feels like to be a creative artist who is also a woman, a woman of intellect and passion, to whom both are equally necessary, growing from childhood through adolescence to the threshold of full adulthood.'[39] Joan Lidoff writes that it is to these two novels that 'we must turn for the inner truths Stead herself would find most important about her life.'[40]

An autobiographical reading of *The Man* and *For Love Alone* makes Stead's understanding of her own life the object of the reading. This has had several important consequences. First, it has brought attention to these two novels at the expense of Stead's other works, and this in turn has obscured both the continuities and the differences among them—her repeated returns to the obsessions and imprisonments of family life and sexual relations, and yet the variety of fictional modes within which she explores these themes. Secondly, then, while we look for continuities which will help us to characterize Stead's writing and to learn to read her texts, we tend to ignore the prodigious variety of the narrative experiments she set herself. Feminists, in particular, have tended to characterize her as a novelist of liberation, and so our readings of her non-heroic women characters in other texts have often been reductive or even nonplussed. Thirdly, she has been seen by most critics, feminist and non-feminist, as a certain kind of realist, one for whom the 'authenticity of experience' is paramount over either literary or political complexity. Consequently, moral-psychological readings have predominated over those which emphasize the social and ideological contexts inscribed in the fiction and its distinctive modes of narrative structure and textual play.

Stead's insistence on the (auto)biographical truth of

her fiction has been employed to authorize certain readings and render others illegitimate. As a way of undermining the authoritative status of this authorial persona, we might return it to the interviews in which it is constructed, and read *them* as texts. Interviews are structures of literary discourse, repertoires of questions and indeed answers whose terms inevitably derive from contemporary critical and political preoccupations. The interview could be compared in some respects to the confession as described by Foucault: 'The confession is a ritual of discourse in which the speaking subject is also the subject of the statement: it is also a ritual which unfolds within a power relationship.' It is an historically specific form of avowal where the individual, instead of being vouched for by others, became 'authenticated by the discourse of truth he was able or obliged to pronounce concerning himself'.[41] Foucault's analysis incidentally brings together terms from two different roots which bear on this question: *auto*, as in autobiography and authentic; and *auctor*, as it occurs in author and authority.

The interview involves a reversal of the confession's power relationship; but it also has an individualizing effect.[42] The interview can be seen as the dominant mode by which her public can come to 'know' an author by that author's own apparently unmediated accounts of herself rather than by means of literary authorities vouching for her. Yet when these spontaneous self-descriptions are compared one with another, credibility is sorely tried by the manifest inconsistencies and self-contradictions on certain topics (for instance, her anecdotes about composition and memories of the novels themselves). Analysed as textual constructions, however, they produce an 'authorial myth', a story about how she came to be as she is.[43] It is the repetition, the re-telling of the basic stories of her authorial myth, and the uses made of it by critics, that render the interview, in the case of Christina Stead, so powerful a means of setting up the image of the 'author' as described by Barthes:

> The *author* still reigns in histories of literature, in biographies of writers, interviews, magazines.... The image of literature to be found in ordinary culture is tyrannically centred on the author, his person, his life, his tastes, his passions.... The *explanation* of a work is always sought in the man or woman who produced it, as if it were always in the end, through the more or less transparent allegory of the fiction, the voice of a single person, the *author* 'confiding' in us.[44]

Barthes is of course not talking about a personal 'tyranny' but a discursive one: the dominant way of talking about literature, which moves along a con- tinuum from academic literary criticism to newspaper reviewing, refers all meaning back to a single image or persona of 'the author'. It is a move which homogenizes writers at the very moment it claims to individualize them: each one is discursively constructed after a common model of subjectivity which locates creativity as the originating impulse and explains all the fictions produced as results or realizations of particular kinds of experiences (notably, experiences of trauma or inspi- ration).[45] It is this explanatory move, this 'author criticism', which produces the 'allegorizing' of fiction as the author's confidences which Barthes characterizes in the passage I have quoted. Neither Barthes, writing of 'the death of the author', nor Foucault, asking 'What is an Author?', is saying that there is no such thing as an author: they are talking about a myth, an ideological function, not a total fallacy.[46]

Nevertheless it might seem to run counter to the whole project of feminist criticism to urge with Barthes that 'it is language which speaks, not the author',[47] even though his argument seeks to establish the power of the reader. Foucault's development of the argument in 'What is an Author?' allows him to conclude 'What does it matter who is speaking?', whereas feminist critics have been at pains to point out that women and other Others are positioned *differently* from the dominant masculine subject of discourses, and in Nancy Miller's words:

> The removal of the Author has not so much made room for a revision of the concept of authorship as it has, through a variety of rhetorical moves, repressed and inhibited discussion of any writing identity in favour of the (new) monolith of anonymous textuality, or 'transcendental anonymity'.[48]

Yet we need not baulk, I think, at Foucault's more moderate and historically specific formulation of the problem of author-criticism, that what we are looking at is the 'author function',the 'idea of an author which creates a specific kind of intelligibility for works of literature',[49] for that function depends on a concept of the unified subject which is much in dispute in contemporary thought, including some feminisms. We do, however, need to question various practices within the field of feminist criticism, and the extent to which they are committed to and limited by 'author criticism' of the kind described here.

'Lives of Modern Women'

In choosing to devote almost half of my study to analyses of *The Man Who Loved Children* and *For Love Alone*, I do not want to repeat the gesture of author-criticism but rather to read these novels for their exploration of the ways female subjectivity is culturally inscribed. The first of them offers to feminist theory, I argue, a fable of the 'feminine Oedipus complex', achieved through the interaction between the novel's account of a girl's sexual coming-of-age and her own play about 'The Tragedy of the Snake-Man, or Father'. The second novel I read as a more historical placing of the young woman's rebellion against the father and patriarchal social relations beyond the family. In both, my reading aims to emphasize the social and political texturing of those processes, and the specifically literary strategies involved in structuring the relations of (woman) reader and representations of women. I want then to extend these considerations to Stead's other woman-centred texts, the satirical or at least anti-heroic portraits, *Letty Fox* and *Miss Herbert*, and the heretically 'political' novels, *Cotters' England* and *I'm Dying Laughing*.

There are many possible groupings of her fictions, of course; in selecting her novels about women's lives I am appropriating them for a feminist analysis which aims at depth rather than breadth—for there are already two introductory feminist studies which cover all her fiction. 'Lives' serves as a name for this grouping, and does not indicate a particular literary mode such as biography. It is a category derived from Stead's own comment that she was intrigued by the idea of a series of tales about the 'lives of the obscure'.[50] While most of her characters could be said to fall into this category, it seems a particularly appropriate epithet for the lives of women—indeed, Virginia Woolf refers in *A Room of One's Own* to 'the obscure lives of women', suggesting both their hidden sexual desires and their material poverty.[51] And poor and obscure women are the subject of Teresa Hawkins' first story in *For Love Alone*. The idea of a series of stories on the stages of a woman's life seems to have haunted Stead, for there are several such schema among her unpublished manuscripts: 'A Natural History of Women' was one; another was a novel entitled 'More Lives Than One'.[52] A different version of this idea was perhaps the anthology of prose fiction edited by Stead and William Blake, *Modern Women in Love*, which they proposed at one stage to develop into a series of television programmes. Her evident admiration for Balzac's writing and his vast *Comédie Humaine* may also have contributed to the idea of a series of interlocking fictions. Although I would not wish to argue that her published tales of modern women constitute a series in this sense, her abiding interest in what people make of the circumstances of their lives and in 'the psychological drama of the person' would support a grouping of her stories around the shared circumstance of womanhood in modern capitalist society.

So complex and obscure are Stead's 'modern women' that the intentionally anachronistic epithet is strongly tinged with irony. Indeed, I see her as the great ironist of women's experience in the postwar world. She produced in her fiction a remarkable range of women characters complete with all the contradictions between their social subordination and their personal will to survive. They are historically representative, as I hope to show, but never offered as morally exemplary for either good or bad: her commitment to observe without prescribing human behaviour, as a 'naturalist', results in a sometimes dizzying lack of narrative direction on these matters. Never simply victims, and hardly heroines in any conventional sense, her 'modern women' both contest and comply with cultural definitions of femininity.

'Reading woman' in these texts provides a way of exploring some of the implications of the new conception of the subject which Teresa de Lauretis sees emerging in contemporary feminist writing, a notion of identity which is 'not the goal but rather the point of departure of the process . . . by which one begins to know that and how the personal is political':

> It is neither, in short, the imaginary identity of the individualist bourgeois subject, which is male and white; nor the 'flickering' of the posthumanist Lacanian subject, which is too nearly white and at best (fe)male. What is emerging in feminist writings is, instead, the concept of a multiple, shifting, and often self-contradictory identity, a subject not divided in, but rather at odds with, language; an identity made up of heterogeneous and heteronomous representations of gender, race, and class, and often indeed across languages and cultures. . .[53]

Reading Stead's fiction from such a feminist position can produce not only evidence of this process but new ways of understanding it—fiction is part of feminist theory, in this respect.

Chapter Two

The Patriarchal Family Drama: The Man Who Loved Children

The single-minded intensity of its evocation of domestic terror gives it a greater artistic cohesion than Stead's subsequent work, which tends towards the random picaresque. And Stead permits herself a genuinely tragic resolution. The ravaged harridan, Henny, the focus of the novel, dies in a grand, fated gesture, an act of self-immolation that, so outrageous has been her previous suffering, is almost a conventional catharsis. One feels that all Henny's previous life has been a preparation for her sudden, violent departure from it and, although the novel appals, it also, artistically, satisfies, in a way familiar in art. Later, Stead would not let her readers off the hook of life so easily. She won't allow us the dubious consolations of pity and terror again.[1]

Angela Carter proposes that *The Man Who Loved Children* acquired the 'romantic reputation of a unique master-piece' because its artistic cohesion grants it the force and magnitude of a Greek tragedy. The reading I want to develop takes up this association with Greek tragedy but construes it differently, as a kind of feminine Oedipus, a modern fable about the female subject's emergence from the patriarchal family. Such a reading, by shifting focus from Henny, the wife and mother, to Louisa, the daughter, extends beyond tragic pity and terror to encompass utopian desire and power.

A family 'unhappy in a way almost unbelievably their own', wrote Randall Jarrell, echoing Tolstoy, in his influential Introduction to the 1965 reissue of this novel. Feminist critics, myself included, have also seen the family as the novel's subject, but have disputed the claim that it is unique, arguing that its power dynamics are characteristic of the modern patriarchal family form. Carter names Stead as 'one of the great articulators of family life', of 'families that are in a terminal state of malfunction'. But while she regards The Man as Henny's tragedy, others pay more attention to the eldest daughter's escape from the family, and read the novel's resolution as one more weighted to the heroic and utopian than the tragic. In this way it has been read as a variation on the Bildungsroman, the novel of development, but a variation which gives, distinctively, more weight and scope to the family and its internal dynamics than to the individual subject who emerged from it in the end. Such a reshaping of the classic nineteenth-century bourgeois form of the Bildungsroman, in particular Louie's rejection of her family life and her search for an alternative, has been read by Marxist critic Terry Sturm as a critical exploration of Engels' proposition that the modern family is the 'cellular form of civilized society, in which the nature of the oppositions and contradictions fully active in that society can be studied'.[3] Extending this, a feminist reading such as my own can emphasize the patriarchal nature of the nuclear family and the historical struggle of the daughter to emerge, beyond its repetitions, as an independent subject.[4] The tension between an historical and a psychoanalytic reading of the novel's representation of family dynamics will, I hope, prove to be a productive one.

Personal History, Social History

The parallels with Stead's own life are very close, and well known: her mother died when she was an infant and for some time she and her father lived with his sister (on whom Bonnie in the novel is modelled) and her small daughter. Her father David Stead, a self-educated scientist employed by the state government Fisheries Board, married again, when Christina was five, to Ada Gibbons. They lived at Lydham Hill in Bexley, south of Sydney, a house owned by Ada's wealthy father, and there she had six children in ten years. When Christina was fifteen the family moved to Watson's Bay, on Sydney Harbour, and she completed her secondary education at Sydney Girls' High School. The parallels between Sam Pollit and her father are considerable: David Stead made a trip to England in 1915 to buy trawlers for the state fishing fleet which he had instituted, but two years after his return was ousted from his position as general manager of the state trawling industry. In 1921–3 he served as Acting Director of Food Supplies for the British government in Malaya. He was a well-known conservationist and as a supporter of the Australian Labor Party, an advocate of 'state socialism'.[5]

Critics taking on an autobiographical reading (under Stead's guidance, it must be said), have neglected until recently the novel's implied historical and cultural analysis. These dimensions of the fiction come into view when one registers the transposition in place and time of the autobiographical material in the making of the novel. Stead's own comment was always that this had been done to 'protect the family' (and it appears that her father never did read the novel), but she did more than change the locale from Sydney to Baltimore and Washington, DC. She also changed the historical time of the story to the late 1930s, nearly a quarter of a century later than the equivalent period in her own life. That had been a time marked, for Australians, by the massacre of troops at Gallipoli (and subsequently the initiation of a national legend) as well as by fierce debates over the conscription of soldiers and, ultimately, the strength of colonial ties with Britain. The time of the novel, however, coincides with the build-up to World War Two in Europe, Roosevelt's New Deal and the expansion of US influence in the Pacific (to which Sam Pollit's membership of the Anthropological Mission to Malaya and Manila for the Smithsonian Institute alludes). In the second political context, the ideas attributed to Sam, and which David Stead had held in a very different time and place, about the superior democracy of New World governments, about meritocracy and the virtues of centralized state control, about world peace and about the possibilities of 'social improvement' through eugenics, take on different and more sinister connotations.[6] Thus the transposition in time of the novel's events sharpens its representation of domestic tyranny and extends it to the nation and the rest of the world.

Jose Yglesias has declared that when *The Man Who Loved Children* appeared in 1940 it was impossible to ignore the fact that it was a 'profoundly political work'. He describes its setting as the time of Roosevelt's second term, when 'Marxists were not revolutionaries and liberals were not pessimists'.[7] Following this, Jonathan Arac reads the novel as a critique of 'the popular front rhetoric' of the period, and Samuel Clemens Pollit as Stead's 'composite figure of Charles Dickens and Mark Twain as petty-bourgeois *pater familias* and socialist booster of the 1930s'.[8] The public ramifications of Sam's *paterfamilias* role had their precedent in Roosevelt himself, as Jennifer McDonell has argued, quoting testimony to the President's 'mastery of radio technique': 'that reassuring voice, at every crisis for more than a dozen years, penetrated millions of home ...'[9]

At the end of the novel, when his wife is dead and his eldest and once-favourite child is about to flee the family circle, Sam pursues his ambition to have a radio programme of his own. His friends

> thought either foreign affairs or the children's hour would suit him, but he himself thought of himself as 'Uncle Sam'.... On his Uncle Sam Hour, he would tell not only folk tales that had been handed down from our forefathers, things devised in their frontier nights after hand-to-hand battles with hardship, and distorted tales brought over from crooked old Europe, but also tales of our revolutionary past, high deeds of stern men and brave women whereby we won the freedom we have...
>
> He had always said that though, no doubt, Jesus Christ had never existed, the idea of a 'second coming' was a touching illustration of mankind's wish for uplift and regeneration; and that if a real saviour ever came, he would come over the radio. (pp. 515—16)

The conflation of the Voice of America and the Messiah mockingly measures the extent of Sam's monomania (his daughter's accusation, p.85). Yet this figure's sheer capacity for survival is a crucial element of the novel's ending. Its beginning, too, featured one of Sam's self-representations as a man of power, this time a more conventional individualist with a long American tradition behind him:

'Going to glory', said Sam: 'I've come a long way, a long, long, way, Brother. Eight thousand a year and expenses—and even Tohoga House, in Georgetown, D.C., lovely suburb of the nation's capital; and the children of poor Sam Pollit, bricklayer's son, who left school at twelve, are going to university soon, under the flashing colonnades of America's greatest city, in the heart of the democratic Athens, much greater than any miserable Athens of the dirt-grubbers of antiquity, yes—I feel sober, at rest. . . .' 'By Gemini', he thought, taking a great breath, 'this is how men feel who take advantage of their power'. (p.54)

Reality seems to confirm his constitutional optimism, his success validating the American dream passed on to him by his mother 'who came from the good old days when mothers dreamed of their sons' being President.'

His dream of power is, he thinks, innocent of personal vanity, devoted to the service of mankind. As his thoughts drift on to that other dream of power, his relations with women, the writing makes the first of its many shifts back forth between political and personal power, between socially defined and individually experienced desires:

'Another thing', said Sam to himself, 'is that going away now, Madeleine and I will have time to use our heads, get things straight: the love that harms another is not love—but what desires beset a man! . . . We must not be carried away. We each have too much to lose.' He strode on, 'Forget, forget!' He struggled to remember something else, something cheerful. . . . There was a young creature there, timid, serious, big-eyed. . . . What an innocent, attentive face! It positively flamed with admiration; and the child-woman's name was Gillian. . . .

'By Gee', he exclaimed half-aloud, 'I am excited! A pity to come home to a sleeping house, and what's not asleep is the devil incarnate; but we're a cheerful bunch, the Pollits are a cheerful bunch . . .' (p.55)

The grouping of female figures is symptomatic of the patriarchal power he embodies: the temptation of passionate love, which must be repressed for 'we have too much to lose'; the child-woman's adoration of his knowledge and power; and the 'devil incarnate', Henny, the mother of his children, who hates him but whom he cannot afford to let go. The moral rhetoric he favours is high Victorian, but he is also master of scientific discourse and of a comic mixture of Mark Twain and Artemus Ward with which he talks to the children.

It might appear that only the man's, the father's, construction is discursively marked as culturally and historically specific. Thus Jarrell characterizes Henny in universalist terms as 'one of those immortal beings in whom the tragedy of existence is embodied',[10] who represents 'natural outlawry of womankind', in the novel's words (p.275). Yet a feminist reader, wary of ascriptions of the 'eternal feminine' whether angelic or diabolic, can discern traces of historical specificity in the descriptions of Henny as an 'old-fashioned woman', a woman with no place in public life but who, rather, 'belonged' to her house as she belonged to her marriage: 'Though she was a prisoner in it, she possessed it' (p.45). Her function in the public world has been as an object of exchange between men, for her wealthy father, 'a self-made man who loved struggling talent, picked out ... Samuel Pollit and made him his son-in-law and advanced him' (p.208). (To establish Sam as a scientist in the state bureaucracy might be seen as a kind of investment of private sector capital in the public sector.) Henny, like the women castigated by home economics experts since the late nineteenth century, is not trained for service in the modern nuclear family. In her case, she has been educated in the grand-bourgeois manner to the expectation of a wealthy marriage, servants, and the social life for which her 'ladylike' accomplishments of music and sewing were intended. She is a magnificently bad manager of the household, and runs up large debts which, without an income from her father's estate, she can never repay.

She can also be read as a representative married woman, whatever her class:

> For it was not Henny alone who went through this inferno, but every woman, especially, for example, Mrs Wilson, the woman who came to wash every Monday. Mrs Wilson, too, 'big as she was, big as an ox', was insulted by great big brutes of workmen, with sweaty armpits, who gave her a leer, and Mrs Wilson, too, had to tell grocers where they got off, and she too had to put little half-starved cats of girls, thin as toothpicks, in their places. (p.47)

The examples are well chosen, for the respectable married woman, whether she is Mrs Wilson or Henrietta Collyer Pollit, has to defend herself against male sexual aggression, keep the family's financial head above water, and defend monogamy against the 'cats of girls' who threaten it: marriage is an oppressive and tenuous security, but it is all they have. The difference is that Henny's youth was closer to the romanticized model and now, a veritable Madame Bovary, she reads romantic novels and takes a lover, a gormless bachelor called Bert who appears, briefly but unforgettably in the novel, in his 'moral BVD's'. In Henny's 'old-fashioned woman', 'child-chained and house-confined' in marriage, can also be traced the loosening of rigid Victorian class/ gender distinctions between 'ladies' and 'women' and their appropriate codes of sexual behaviour. Now there is only a difference in degree of poverty, it seems: Mrs Pollit and Mrs Wilson are economically dependent and socially controlled, and their controllers include other women. She is a modern woman, she has the vote, Henny reflects:

> But the fact remains that a man can take my children from me if he gets something on me; and a lot of fat old maids and scrawny hags in their fifties stand back of every darn man-made law in this and any other state. I have to be pure and chaste before getting married and after—for whom please?—for Samuel Pollit; otherwise, I'm no good before and he can take my children after. (p.165)

Much as she loathes Sam, Henny is obliged to conceal the fact that she has a lover, because to do so would be to lose the children. Subsequent events suggest that she is already pregnant by him. Looking at her wedding ring, she vows to exploit the only power she has over Sam, 'the dread power of wifehood':

> If this plain ugly link meant an eyeless eternity of work and poverty and an early old age, it also meant that to her alone this potent breadwinner owed his money, name, and fidelity, to her, his kitchenmaid and body servant. For a moment, after years of scamping, she felt the dread power of wifehood . . . (p.173)

So Henny makes no reply when Sam makes his appalling confession that the 'sole reason' for his insistence on their marriage continuing, 'despite my sorrow and without your love', was his hope that 'I would produce mighty children, a tribe of giants to come after me' (the practical eugenicist speaking). And when he begs her to go to him, to 'have another child, the seal of all our sorrows', to 'let this be our fortress against the world', she complies, silently vowing to 'wring every penny of my debts out of him some way, before he goes' (p.176). Henny is obliged to be immoral, breaking man-made laws. Because she is subject to this morality and without any alternative of her own, she inevitably sees life as a projection of herself, corrupt and 'rotten', and this is evident in the language of her many tirades.

Contradictions specific to the modern middle-class nuclear family are expressed in Henny, and also in the novel's portrayal of the children's upbringing. The position of the children in the family is marked by powerlessness, a lack of autonomy which first Louie and then Ernie, as they approach adolescence, realize. Thus Ernie, reflecting on the subject closest to his heart, money, realizes that adults who forbid the mention of money as impolite are merely handing down 'pious precepts' aimed at keeping the young out of their game. He sees that these are 'all commands enforced by power alone and obeyed by weakness alone', and observes that:

> as Louie grew up, she obeyed less and less, not letting things slip by inadvertence or sly disobedience, but refusing to do things in open revolt—'I will not because it is not right!' Now, Louie had her own right and wrong, she was already entering their world of power. (p.140)

Their upbringing is authoritarian, father-centred and home-focused, but not comparable with Victorian families extended by servants or relatives. It is not child-centred in that distinctively twentieth-century U S way, but depends on the benevolent despotism of the father: it is his authority specifically that the adolescents reject. Their activities, organized in regimental fashion by Sam, are recognizably suburban (repair and maintenance of the house and garden) as well as the educational activities deemed proper by their scientist father. The home-centredness of their lives suggests either a poorer family, or an earlier era, for they go to no public entertainments or sports, nor do they visit other families. School is the only alternative world they know—and Sam identifies the school as inimical to his authority, dreaming of abolishing school for children like his and forming them into 'communities with a leader' (p.361).

At first glance, Louie seems, like Henny, to be without particular historical 'placing' or context. Her ambitions are rarely specified beyond the level of 'If I did not know I was a genius I would kill myself—why live?'. Critics who would read Louie's situation as the timeless one of the genius-to-be[11] are encouraged by her self-characterizations as the ugly duckling (p.94) or the legendary changeling. Her admiration for great men—and they are the great rebels of the high Romantic period, mostly—is not specific to her time, or her gender. Yet it provides her with a powerful discourse to use against Sam: her admiration for Nietzsche is absolutely right in terms of this rebellion, for it sets up the prophet of will against the Darwinian; she quotes the man who challenged the self-evidence of the laws of cause and effect against her father's hero, Darwin, that apotheosis of nineteenth-century deterministic science.[12]

Other aspects of Louie's characterization which may seem anachronistic in the 1930s setting can equally be marshalled in support of a reading which places her rebellion in a longer historical perspective. Her dream of an alternative way of living is furnished by visits to her dead mother's family, the Bakens, at Harpers Ferry— and that is hardly a 1930s decor. The Bakens are associated with the God of the Old Testament, and with the emancipatory ideals of the Union. They are poor and proud, but not ambitious and quarrelsome like the Pollits: their home town (and emancipationist ideals?) has become a backwater and they are impoverished as a result (p.178). But she gets from her Baken relatives not only a measure of Christian sweetness and light ('prayers and family love, weakminded and backward') to counteract the tough times at home. She also gets a crucial *grounding* that is both literal and, metaphorically, a grounding in history that implicitly challenges the eternal present tense constructed by Sam's scientific discourse:

> [T]he placid, high-minded heavens of Pollitry were rolled up and there was a landscape to the far end of the sky—an antique, fertile, yeoman's country, where, in the shelter of other customs and tribal gods, people believing themselves to be the children of God stuck to their occupations, gave praise, and accompanied their humblest deeds with the thunder of mystic song. (p.186)

Her resistance to the attempt by her best friend, Clare, to 'get Louie to be a socialist and to read *Progress and Poverty*' (p.350), because she is so engrossed with adoration of her schoolteacher, is also incidentally a resistance to interesting herself in areas close to Sam's expertise and an affirmation of herself as an artist, 'mad with love'. As she writes to Clare:

> Everyone thinks I am sullen, sulky, surly, grim; but I am the two hemispheres of Ptolemaic marvels, I am lost Atlantis risen from the sea, the Western Isles of infinite promise, the apples of the Hesperides and daily make the voyage to Cytherea, island of snaky trees and abundant shade with leaves large and dripping juice, the fruit that is my heart, but I have a thousand hearts hung on every tree, yes, my heart drips along every fence paling. (p.439)

The literature and legend of the past is Louie's only alternative to her father's mediation of the public world: it is the ammunition of her rebellion and the motive force that sustains her.

Feminist Readings of the Daughter's Rebellion

Feminist critics interested in the daughter's rebellion, but without attending to the novel's historical dimension, tend to resort to psychological models to explain it. A potentially feminist reading of the novel from a position close to Stead's own is offered in Dorothy Green's essay, 'Storm in a Teacup'. She reads it as an 'ecological novel':

> a struggle for survival in a habitat which is too small and impoverished for the 'fighting fish' it contains. The dominant male survives in it, his mate succumbs, but his daughter...manages to fight her way out of this closed ecosystem and goes for a walk 'round the world' to find a new one in which she can flourish more easily.[13]

In this familial closed system, she argues, the battle—its origins, the combatants, the strategy, the tactics—is universal. It is that of the artist struggling to be born. This is a familiar and convincing exemplar of the *Kunstlerroman* reading, but it is gender-blind, paying no particular attention to the fact of the protagonist's being female: it is the uniqueness of the artist which is considered important, rather than her shared cultural fate as a woman. The problem with an ecological model of the human micro-system of the family is, of course, its limitation as an analogy: the family is an aquarium rather than an ocean, confining 'human beasts' in conditions in which the dominance of the dominant Pollit male derives from his access to economic, legal and ideological power, as breadwinner, husband and scientist respectively, while the 'biological weakness' of the female, who is prematurely aged by incessant childbearing, is exacerbated by factors external to, but defining of the marriage: her economic dependence, her fear of the law's reprisals against erring wives and her lack of access to a discourse socially powerful enough to combat the scientist and public orator. Green's gesture towards women like Henny, 'conditioned to be dependent',[14] cannot encompass such *material* determinants of male dominance and female subordination, and it shares this limitation with all liberal humanist feminisms which depend on moral and psychological explanations of women's oppression, and therefore envisage only individual liberation by will.

Such feminist emphases on women as victims of male aggression and the validity of their anger came to coexist, by the 1980s, with an insistence on the value of qualities conventionally attributed to women—nurturance, endurance, sensitivity. At its most complex, criticism based on this feminist position involves negotiating the intricate relations between stereotypes, their ideological underpinnings, their social and historical contexts and their impingement on individual women's self-constructions—hence the importance of literary 'evidence' of the female experience when it is conceptualized in this way.

It is in this context that I want to discuss Joan Lidoff's reading of *The Man* because it intelligently highlights the *textual* implications of a feminist emphasis on the horrors of the female experience in marriage and domesticity. Not satisfied with the usual critical generalizations about the way the novel contrasts Sam's rational moral and scientific discourse with Henny's dark tirades, Lidoff specifies what Henny has in common with all Stead's characters and what her particular 'imagery of anger' signifies about women's social and psychic lives.

> Henny's metaphoric failure to distinguish her feelings from the world outside herself derives from a way of perceiving that colours all of a character's environment with the suffocating reflections of her own fantasies.... Stead uses

grotesque metaphors as objective correlatives of her characters' distress – pulling all the created universe into the shapes of the fears, angers, desires of their inner lives.[15]

It is not clear, however, how one might distinguish the 'grotesque imagery which blurs boundaries to threaten us with recognition of the immanence of chaos' from the specifically feminine form of the 'domestic Gothic' which at once derives from women's 'relational' rather than 'autonomous' self-definitions and dwells on dirt, disorder, physicality, sexual ambivalence.

This contradiction between claiming the Domestic Gothic for female psychology and characterizing *all* of Stead's characters as manifestations of the grotesque and its boundary confusions is apparently resolved by Lidoff's discussion of Louisa. Noting that she shares with Henny the vision of a polarized world of victims and oppressors, Lidoff points out that she constructs for herself 'an equally exaggerated heroic self-image' fit to defeat the tyrannical power which she imagines her father wielding. But as well, 'Louie's Gothic sensibility is also Stead's narrative voice. The violence that permeates life and death, sex and conversation, for the Pollits becomes part of Louie's world view and that of the novel itself.'[16] The collapsing together of narrative voice, the novel's world-view, its hero and its major victim into the Domestic Gothic finally overloads the concept. It begins to sound like a normative theory of the feminine aesthetic, of the one expressive form best suited to the female psyche, rather than a particular mode of writing.[17]

An analysis of Stead's fiction that is more centrally informed by US feminist theory is Judith Kegan Gardiner's. Her general concern has been to account for what is distinctive about twentieth-century women's fiction by drawing on psychological and psychoanalytic theories of female identity formation, especially those of Nancy Chodorow and Dorothy Dinnerstein which affirm the centrality of the mother-daughter bond in this process, and its difference from models of male identity formation. *The Man Who Loved Children* has been a key text in several of Gardiner's essays in relation to the themes of the death of the mother in women's fiction, and of 'the heroine as her author's daughter' (the title of her new book on Rhys, Lessing and Stead). The earlier discussion begins by quoting Adrienne Rich's definition of 'matrophobia' as 'the fear not of one's mother or of motherhood but of *becoming one's mother*' (emphasis in original). This fear is seen as both experiential and mythical: a vertiginous blurring of ego boundaries between mother and daughter on the one hand, and a rejection of the mother as symbol of one's cultural fate as a woman on the other. The hostility between mothers and daughters is gratified, argues Gardiner, by fictional 'plots that painfully murder the heroines' mothers while they pacify our guilt because the deaths all arise from "natural" causes within the narrative framework.'[18]

In the case of *The Man*, however, it is not the plot but the heroine who kills the mother. Gardiner refers to the 'mythic clarity' with which Stead represents matricidal rage: 'Henny is not the one whom Louie most hates, but she is the mirror of what Louie must not become, and so she must be killed.'[19] Stead's text provides the limit case for Gardiner's matricide thesis, and even takes on the dimension of fable or myth—killing the 'wicked' stepmother, defying the father, asserting her independence in heroic terms.

On the level of realism, Gardiner's account of the mother-daughter relationship is less satisfactory. A kind of intuitive female bond does indeed grow between them as Louie nears her menarche[20] and it is also an alliance against Sam:

This creature that was forming against the gay-hearted, generous, eloquent, goodfellow was bristly, foul, a hyena, hater of woman the house-jailed and child-chained against the key-carrier, childnamer, and riot-haver'. (p.72)

At the same time they remain deeply divided by their different relations to him, the patriarch. Henny is always ready to abuse Louie as a way of attacking Sam:

> She wanted to know whether Sam knew that his beautiful genius' clothes were smeared with filth and that most of the time the great big overgrown wretch with her great lolloping breasts looked as if she'd rolled in a pigsty or a slaughterhouse, and that she couldn't stand the streams of blood that poured from her fat belly... (p.442)

It is precisely Louie's coming of age that underlines Henny's exhaustion from child-bearing and her marriage bitterness, and it occasions some of vilest abuse. Louie, for her part, is horrified by Henny's violence, frightened by her homicidal threats, yet she also acts with the same sort of practical kindness towards her stepmother as she does towards the younger children. But most importantly, in relation to this question of the bonds between women, she is at some level indifferent to Henny, whose affection she never expects and never attempts to win.[21] What daughterly guilt she experiences is in relation to the father, not to the mother—a point which I shall return to.

In relation to the maternal metaphor of female authorship, 'the heroine as her author's daughter', Gardiner sums up: 'bonds between women structure the deepest layer of female personality and establish the patterns to which literary identifications are analogous.'[22] In this current of feminist theory, the interest in mother–daughter bonds and identification is vitally linked to the political imperative to elaborate the grounds on which women can struggle collectively to end their oppression—there are political and spiritual as well as literary analogies of identification at stake here. And there is a strong tendency in such writing to idealize the mother-daughter bond and its supposed consequences. Take, for instance, Gardiner's account of Chodorow (whose work has been enormously influential among U S feminist philosophers and sociologists as well as literary critics):

> First, a girl forms her gender identity positively, in becoming like the mother with whom she begins life in a symbiotic merger. Second, she must develop in such a way that she can pleasurably re-create the mother-infant symbiosis when she herself becomes a mother. As a result, women develop capacities for nurturance, dependence and empathy more easily than men do and are less threatened by these qualities, whereas independence and autonomy are typically harder for women to attain.[23]

Such a general statement raises a major problem to do with reading Stead's novel: does the fact that such a normative description does not fit the fictional representation mean that Louie is to be considered an exception and—again—a 'portrait of the artist' rather than a woman? In order to understand the shared as well as the specific elements in this representation of a young woman, we shall require a more complex model, and one which gives a function to the paternal as well as to the maternal figure in the formation of female subjectivity.

Teresa de Lauretis, discussing the operation of desire in narrative in psychoanalytic terms, offers an alternative model of gendered subjectivity. Taking up Freud's view that 'femininity' and 'masculinity' are never fully attained or fully relinquished, she argues that 'the two terms ... do not refer so much to qualities or states of being inherent in a person, as to positions which she occupies in relation to desire. They are terms of identification.'[24] In narrative terms, the masculine position is that of the mythical subject and the feminine is the mythical obstacle or, simply, the space in which narrative movement occurs. Feminine and masculine, as positions occupied in relation to desire, correspond respectively to the passive and the active aims of the libido—the desire for the other, and the desire to be desired by the other. This is, Lauretis concludes, 'the operation by which narrative and cinema solicit the spectators' consent and seduce women into femininity: by a double identification, a surplus of pleasure...'[25] This double identification means, for the female subject, a double desire—for the Mother and for the Father.

We return from this brief foray into classic psycho-analytical theory and semiotics with the makings of a more complex model of psychic formation, where both feminine and masculine identifications are operative, neither being ever fully attained or fully relinquished. Its implication for reading texts is that one 'identifies' not in terms of 'relating to a text as though it were a person'[26] but of interacting with the various subject positions it inscribes in language and ideology. To say this is nevertheless to agree with liberal feminist critics that there are intimate and politically significant links between women writers, women readers and female characters, but it is to complicate the model for conceptualizing these links.

The 'Feminine Oedipus Complex'

Having been deeply influenced in the late 1970s by this US feminist work on the mother–daughter bond and the significance of the pre-Oedipal period in female identity formation, and being struck, like Gardiner, by the 'mythic clarity' with which Stead presents the theme of 'female matricide' in *The Man Who Loved Children*, I set about to explore these themes—and ended up with a triangular and definitely Oedipal 'patriarchal family drama'.[27] My essay addressed questions that surround the daughter's resolution of her Oedipal conflict in relation to the father's desire and the mother's absence (literal, in that her biological mother is dead, and metaphorical, in that the stepmother refuses to stand in the mother's place). Taking off from Green's Darwinian reading of the family as an intra-species struggle for survival, my reading focused particularly on the daughter's sexual coming of age, the mother's horror and the father's fascination with this, arguing that the focus on sexuality sets the struggle within the terms of human culture, that is, of desire and subjectivity rather than mere survival. I attempted to relate an analysis of interpersonal power politics within the family to the central triangular drama between daughter, mother and father as a kind of mythic story; hence the appropriateness of a psychoanalytic framework, derived from Juliet Mitchell's revision of Freud, to theorize desire and subjectivity. I argued that the play within the novel, 'Herpes Rom', could serve as a mythic story of the feminine Oedipus complex, just as Sophocles' 'Oedipus Rex' served Freud.

My argument derives from a focus on Louie and the potential conflict between her coming of age as a woman ('this stupid adolescent crisis', as her father calls it) and her heroic ambitions—if you like, between her feminine and masculine identifications. It is a common subject in women's fiction, often autobiographical, but this novel is one of the few with a utopian ending (perhaps, as Gardiner suggests, because of the mother's death) *and* one of the few in which the daughter's relation to the father is directly addressed and made central.[28] It is

43

curious that even in narratives of feminine destiny which tend to confirm the inevitability of patriarchal power (by denigrating maternal figures, by emphasizing the heroine's defeat, and so on, like Plath's *The Bell Jar*, or the novels of Jean Rhys), the father-daughter relation is rarely explored. It is as if this is taboo. *The Man* suggests why this might be so.

It is in the final third of the novel that this crisis is played out. Henny has refused to take on the traditional maternal role of initiating the adolescent girl into womanhood:

'Why should I go through the rigmarole with another woman's girl? I'm not going to speak to her. It's your place or the place of one of her aunts. I couldn't drag her into all the darn muck of existence myself'. (p. 155)

Although Louie considers it a blessing to be left alone, her father is both fascinated and horrified by

the mystery of female adolescence.... He poked and pried into her life, always with a scientific, moral purpose, stealing into her room when she was absent, noting her mottoes on the wall ... and investigating her linen, shivering with shame when suggestive words came into her mouth. (p. 340)

He would have preferred a 'slim recessive girl whose sex was ashamed'. He fears both her youthful sexuality and her difference from him. He increasingly uses sexual harassment in his bid to maintain control over her, both teasing (ridiculing her writing, her looks, her clumsiness) and threats (that she must protect the children from Henny, and stand by him).

Once Louie had seen him as godlike as he walked beside her and she looked up and beyond him at the enfeebled stars. Thus, for many years, she had seen her father's head, a ghostly earth flame against the heavens, from her little height. (p. 159)

Now she questions his authority and resents his interference. Sam gives her three books for her sexual education: a copy of Shelley, Frazer's *Golden Bough* and a book on wartime atrocities in Belgium. He of course will not discuss them with her, but 'the more she read of these works, the more she felt guilty of a power of her own, and she began suddenly to despise and loathe Sam with an adult passion' (p. 386). At this moment—Stead characteristically juxtaposes events rather than setting them in cause-and-effect order—there is a local scandal: a father is accused of impregnating his young daughter. Sam rants against this 'yellow' press attack on a poor man, 'a father in his own home', declaring that the girl must have lied and that 'every decent-thinking man and decent-living man in this community will be roused by this' (p. 387). The connection thus suggested between Sam's desires and the incest scandal is contiguous with Louie's sense that she had run up against 'an infernal middle kingdom of horror that she alone could stand'. She holds Sam responsible for this vision, and vows silently to take her revenge; at the same time 'against this went her terrible passion for Miss Aiden [her teacher], childish in its ignorance, adult in its turbulency' (p.388). When she reads 'The Cenci' in the volume of Shelley Sam has given her she feels that 'Beatrice was in a case like her'. She learns by heart the lines:

And so my lot was ordered, that a father
First turned the moments of awakening life
To drops, each poisoning youth's sweet hope;...

and recites to Sam the Father's lines referring to Beatrice

as 'this most specious mass of flesh', 'this devil/Which sprung from me as from a hell' but also as 'her bright loveliness...kindled to illumine this dark world' (pp. 389-90). She does not quote Cenci naming himself as 'a fiend, appointed to chastise/The offences of some unremembered world' (The Cenci, IV, ii, 161-2).[29] This line finds its place in Louie's own play, which she writes and has the younger children perform for Sam's fortieth birthday.

This play, 'The Tragedy of the Snake-Man, or Father', is written in English and translated into the language she has devised expressly for it for performance. It has two characters, Anteios the Father and Megara the Daughter; but, although the daughter's name suggests revenge, and the play's prologue, from Longfellow, is: 'Every guilty deed/Holds in itself the seed/Of retribution and undying pain', and though the daughter threatened the father, 'If I could I would hunt you out like the daughters of King Lear', it is nevertheless the Daughter who is killed at the end of this one-act tragedy of 'Herpes Rom':

Father—Anteios and *Daughter*—Megara
ANTEIOS: I must make sure of you. In my eyes you are guilty of a nameless smirch. If I leave you alone for only an hour you sin.
MEGARA: My sin is solitude. My joy too. Yet it is queer in your company only I feel guilty.
ANTEIOS: Naturally! You fear your father.
MEGARA: Fear to be a father and to be hated by your daughter.
ANTEIOS: What have I done?
MEGARA: Every day with rascally wiles you ravish my only joy, my peace of mind. And now my solitude is two. A stranger is there. The name of the stranger is hate. Go, for he would make your eyes bulge out.
ANTEIOS: You are sick, my beloved daughter.

MEGARA: If I could, I would hunt you out like the daughers of King Lear.

ANTEIOS: Horrible: what a she-devil!

MEGARA: (I am) an innocent girl that you have too much plagued. As mother says, I am rotten: but with innocence. If to breathe the sunlight is a sin, what can I do? I see you are determined to steal my breath, my sun, my daylight. The stranger will kill you.

ANTEIOS: What stranger? Are you mad? Kiss me, my daughter.

MEGARA: (Choking) Not me! Help! The stranger strangles me. Thou snake.

ANTEIOS: What stranger? Are you mad? What are you doing? Embrace, kiss me. (Aside) The snake? (He tries to hiss to himself.)

MEGARA: (Shrieking) I am dying. You are the stranger. You are killing me. Murderer! Murderer! Mother!

ANTEIOS: I am only embracing you. My beloved daughter. (But he hisses.)

MEGARA: Mother, father is strangling me. Murderer! (She dies.) (pp. 408–9).

The parallels between Louie's play and 'The Cenci' are there in both the language and the action; the major difference, the fact that Beatrice actually does murder her father, is modified by its consequence—her suicide because she feels his dread power continuing to 'work for me and mine still the same ruin,/Scorn, pain, despair' (Cenci, V, iv, 70-1). The rebellious daughter dies anyway. Interestingly, in Louie's play, it is the power of her own hatred, the 'stranger' with which she threatens her father, that is turned against her: as her father embraces her she cries, choking, 'The stranger strangles me. Thou snake!' The metamorphosis of the Snake Man out of her own stranger/hatred ('alienis', in the code language, suggesting the Latinate term for psycho-analyst, 'alienist') recalls the lines in 'The Cenci' where

Beatrice's mother voices the fear that 'power is as a beast which grasps/And loosens not: a snake whose look transmutes/All things to guilt which is its nutriment' (Cenci IV, iv, 178-80).

The stranger/strangler/snake is the thing exchanged between daughter and father, that grows out of his 'ravishing' her 'only joy, my peace of mind' and that transfers its power to his murderous embrace. The Edenic associations of the snake relate it to sexual guilt and also to the assertion of patriarchal law, both of which are signified by the phallus, an important pre-Christian icon of which is the serpent. Her self-description as 'rotten with innocence' expresses a desire to *know* (as women always do, as Eve did, 'As mother says'). He wishes her to obey, perceiving in her resistance to his gaze only sin, sickness, madness. Like Cenci, he believes himself appointed to 'chastise the offences of some unremembered world'—the world of pre-Oedipal desire, of active sexuality on the part of the girl. The punishment for her resistance to the Father's regulation of those desires—indeed, to the institution of patriarchal law, of the Law—is death. The mother's absence from the play—she does not appear in response to the daughter's cries for help—implies that she has already submitted to this death as an autonomous female being, submitted to the law and become a wife and a mother. Thus Louie's play could be said to enact the nullification of female subjectivity demanded by the feminine resolution of the Oedipus complex: the conversion of her active sexual desire to a passive aim, and her submission to patriarchal law.

A feminist understanding of what is at stake in this resolution, taken as a fable of female subjectivity under patriarchy, might be one which accepts the pattern outlined by Freud but radically questions its meaning. Luce Irigaray's essay, 'The Blind Spot of an Old Dream of Symmetry' is one such reading of Freud. Its title refers to the Freudian project of formulating a single law of psychic development which would explain feminine and masculine subjectivities as symmetrical opposites. This very project, argues Irigaray, is defined by the masculine subject's blindness to female sexuality, reading its difference from the male as lack (castration) rather than a specific, a different sexuality; the masculine subject's blindness is definitive because this—and 'every theory of the "subject"'—is formulated from within phallocentric discourse.[30] With reference to the daughter's relationship to the father, as Jane Gallop explains the implications of Irigaray's critique of Freud:

> If the phallus is the standard of value, then the Father, possessor of the phallus, must desire the daughter in order to give her value. But the Father is a man...and cannot afford to desire otherness, an other sex, because that opens up his castration anxiety. The father's refusal to seduce the daughter, to be seduced by her (seduction wreaking havoc with anal logic and its active/passive distribution), gains him another kind of seduction in the form of the law. The daughter submits to the father's rule, which prohibits the father's desire, the father's penis, out of the desire to seduce the father by doing his bidding and thus pleasing him.[31]

Implicated in this explanation is a radical rethinking of Freud's notorious seduction theory, his conclusion that what female 'hysterics' told him of paternal seduction or sexual abuse was fantasy, not fact, and attributable to their repressed infantile desire for the father. Drawing in particular on Freud's account of Dora, Irigaray and other feminists have pointed to the evidence of countertransference there (of the analyst's desire to be desired by his patient), and have inferred a reciprocal paternal desire for the daughter.[32] It should be pointed out that to define the issue in this way, from within the discourse of

49

psychoanalysis, is by no means to deny or to condone the sexual abuse of children by male relatives but it is to separate the sociological from the psychoanalytical dimensions: the different discourses define their own objects.

A further consequence of Irigaray's psychoanalytic account is that it attributes to the girl an active desire rather than a passive victim role, and thus suggests, at least, some of the complex interactions that result between fantasy and behaviour. Thus she can say:

> [I]t is neither simply true, nor indeed false, to claim that the little girl fantasizes being seduced by her father, since it is equally valid to assume that the father *seduces his daughter* but that, because (in most cases, though not all) he refuses to recognize and live out his desire, *he lays down a law that prohibits him from doing so.* That said, it is his desire which, come what may, prescribes the force, the shape, the modes, etc., of the law he lays down or passes on, a law that reduces to the state of 'fantasy' the little girl's seduced and rejected desire . . .[33]

The wider cultural consequences of this process, as Gallop reads Irigaray, form a vicious circle: 'The daughter desires a heterosexual encounter with the father, and is rebuffed by the rule of the homo-logical, raising the homo over the hetero, the logical over the sexual, decreeing neither the hetero nor the sexual worthy of the father'[34] —a denial of difference and of desire. And the 'anthropological' consequences would break up the neat circuit (as Lévi-Strauss defined it) of incest taboo and exogamy and the exchange of women:

> If the father were to desire his daughter he could no longer exchange her. . . . If you cannot give something up for something of like value, if you consider it nonsubstitutable, then you do not possess it any more than it possesses you.

So the father must not desire the daughter for that threatens to remove him from the homosexual commerce in which women are exchanged between men, in the service of power relations and community for the men.[35]

Louie is bent on refusing the death that her play enacts, and she decides to destroy the situation by killing both parents. Her aim in doing this is to bring to an end the endless repetition of their marital battle, that 'strange Punch-and-Judy show, unrecognizable Sams and Hennys moving in a closet of time, with a little flapping curtain, up and down' (p. 71), but her target might equally well be seen as the endless repetition of desire and denial in the familial triangle. Foiled in this attempt by Henny's final absenting of herself in suicide, Louie later makes a final attempt to show her father the meaning of what has happened. As she had predicted, he refuses to see what she unveiled behind that 'little flapping curtain': 'You don't know what truth is,' Sam rants. 'The truth isn't in you, only some stupid mess of fantasies mixed up with *things I can't even think about*' (p. 519, emphasis added). 'The man who loved children' refuses to understand his own desire, for to acknowledge it would be to undermine the whole cultural edifice of law and morality, with which he is so thoroughly identified, which is raised upon the foundation of that desire's denial. 'He does not understand women or children. He is such a good young man, he is too good to understand people at all,' as his first wife, Louie's mother, had written (p. 520).

Louie throws this line back at him, and it is an accusation of narcissism, the same narcissism which Irigaray diagnoses in phallocentrism. When Louie finally leaves his house, she can see beyond that solipsism whereby everthing is referred back to the man himself: 'She wondered why everyone didn't run away. Things certainly looked different: they were no longer part of herself but objects she could freely consider without prejudice' (p. 522). Yet in order to 'see' like this she has had to commit an 'extreme deed' of self-assertion.

What can be said about this ending in terms of the discourse of psychoanalysis, of the Oedipus complex? Has Louie now enacted a refusal and escape from the feminine identification that is her cultural destiny as a woman? Does her avowal, 'I will be my own mother', amount instead to an identification with Athena, sprung fully-formed from her father's head? In revolting against the Father and setting off for Harper's Ferry and her admired Old Testament grandfather, has she instead taken up a classically masculine position? Certainly, her escape is not part of a feminine identification: she does not think of seeking out the woman she had loved, Miss Aiden, and her friend Clare reluctantly chooses family duty rather than the freedom of the road with Louie. Yet it is as if in leaving her father's house, removing herself from that circuit of exchange, she is freed into an ungendered space, outside of human culture, where she is no longer a clumsy adolescent but takes on the mythic qualities of the dolphin, 'undulating through the waves, one of those beautiful, large, sleek marine mammals that plunged and wallowed, with their clever eyes' (p. 522). The associated images return her to an Edenic scene, 'like the morning of the world': sexually undifferentiated, pre-Oedipal?

For a lyrical moment, perhaps: not for the continuation of her life story, her narrative. The pre-Oedipal space before sexual differentiation, before the establishment of the symbolic order and the law of the Father (in Lacanian terms) has been theorized by Julia Kristeva in a way which relates it to the signifying process and to writing in particular.[36] This process is constituted by the interaction between the symbolic and what Kristeva calls the semiotic, the always-mobile continuum of basic 'pulsions' or pre-Oedipal primary processes. The semiotic 'is anterior to and underlies figurations and therefore also specularization, and only admits analogy with vocal or kinetic rhythm'.[37] Difference, and therefore signification, can only be set in process once this *chora* (the continuous space of the semiotic) is split or separated in the Oedipal phase. The semiotic, repressed, is nevertheless always potentially present; however its association with 'vocal or kinetic rhythm' suggests a different conception of its relation to the symbolic from Freud's unconscious, or Lacan's Imaginary. Its 'appearance' in discourse is characterized not so much in Freudian terms of anti-logic (slips of the tongue, jokes, dreams) but in terms of rhythms (pre-verbal patterns) in movement and sound. Kristeva discusses the work of *avant-garde* writers (all of them male, from Mallarmé to Céline) as effecting disruptions of the symbolic order of discourse which allow access to the semiotic space anterior to it.

Despite her commitment to certain forms of realism, Stead's interest in *chant* (which, she maintained, was the great attraction of Nietzsche's writing for her)[38] and her distinctive use of imagery of movement, of kinaesthesia (particularly evident in *For Love Alone*), both suggest an awareness of the substratum of symbolic language that is analogous to Kristeva's 'semiotic'. In *The Man Who Loved Children* Louie's writing and story-telling feature the grotesque events and surreal logic characteristic of dreams; at the same time, she is fascinated by the rules of language and discourse—wanting to learn Welsh grammar, inventing a language specifically for her play, 'Herpes Rom', the appreciation of genre and conceit shown in her 'Aiden cycle' of poems. This prodigious range of verbal skills may be seen as her major means of contesting Sam's power—and, by extension, patriarchal control—both by beating him at his own game of

Christina Stead

language in the symbolic order and by deploying those verbal resources further so as to draw on the 'semiotic' and thus to signify her own forbidden desires. That is, she contests the Law of the Father with argument, narrative *and* fantasy. Her 'walk around the world' is lyrically utopian because it is in excess of this signifying activity—a grace-note to conclude, granting the narrative a closing figure which seems, paradoxically, to open out onto a whole new world.

Chapter Three

For Love Alone:
A Quest and A Love Story

A literal 'journey around the world' is the subject of Christina Stead's next published novel, *For Love Alone* (1944). Teresa Hawkins, the protagonist, travels from Australia, the 'Island Continent' of Part 1 to the setting of Part 2, 'Port of Registry: London'. As these names already suggest, the novel is shaped around the structure of a journey, and it is marked by kinaesthetic imagery and allusions to many kinds of literary travels. This emphasis on space, place and movement distinguishes the imaginary world of this novel from its predecessor. Where *The Man Who Loved Children* works by repetition, with the horrors of that domestic repetition echoed in the natural imagery that evokes yet other cycles, *For Love Alone* is a work of endless restlessness, of journeying—physical, geographical, intellectual, erotic—and extends to social relations beyond the domestic circle.

Christina Stead

Recasting the Issues

It begins again where *The Man Who Loved Children* left off, in a dramatic scene of the daughter's rebellion against the family patriarch: goaded by his sermonizing and his sexual taunts, Teresa turns on the widowed Andrew Hawkins, threatening, 'I will kill you, father,' while her sister and two brothers look on in mixed horror and amusement.[1] She is an older Louie, a passionate and ambitious young woman, now at the point of entry into adult social and sexual relations: thus the thematic issues around the family are recast. Her heroic stance is also given a different cast, in that she is the narrative's single focus and other characters appear on the scene only to the extent and at the point that they impinge upon her needs and priorities. Around her position at centre stage is grouped a large cast of new characters, most of whom appear only briefly, like the family members, and then move into the background, yielding place to Teresa's lovers.

They all, but especially the lovers, serve to define the kind of world she must come to terms with: as in all of Stead's fiction, they are presented largely through their talk, their monologues, and each of them represents a different kind of discourse on the topics that vitally concern her—sexuality, love, destiny. The father introduces this pattern in the first scene with his hymn to the heavenly harmony of the sexes, mixed with a narcissistic catalogue of his own charms and admirers. But all the other characters' definitions of reality (which are at the same time their self-assertive claims on her attention) are more than matched by Teresa's secret life of fantasy—her reading, art work, daydreams and speculations.

What especially distinguishes this from *The Man Who Loved Children* is the single narrative focus in contrast to

56

the triangular structure of father, mother and daughter/other children in that earlier novel. That shape, and the sense of inevitability about Henny's fate, lends to the novel much of the quality of tragic drama. In contrast the journey shape of *For Love Alone* and its isolated protagonist seeking to be the architect of her own destiny evoke an *epic* form. It certainly fulfils the heroic expectations that are engendered by Louie's final gesture of leaving her father's house to go for a walk around the world, yet it rarely recalls the utopian dimensions of that finale. Teresa's epic journey includes a version of the proposed walk to Harper's Ferry, but that, along with her other ventures, is an ordeal marked by struggle, disappointment, and an outcome quite other than what she had aimed for. Yet it remains heroic in that her aspirations, though modified in detail, are vindicated in their scope. If *The Man Who Loved Children* can be read as the dramatic aspect of Christina Stead's enabling autobiographical myth, *For Love Alone* can be read as its epic phase. Indeed, it evokes, as well as the Homeric epic, many other literary journey structures as well: religious quest, sentimental education, psychological and social *Bildung*, colonial expatriatism, a Joycean flight of the artist and, in the heroine's own words, 'a kind of Darwin's voyage of discovery, as the voyage to Cytherea', to 'our secret desires' (pp. 192–3). But it also 'weaves its epic ambitions', as Lorna Sage puts it, 'into a mock-naive "first novel" format (a young woman's entrance into the world)'.[2]

To the extent that it does evoke this first-novel format, *For Love Alone* deliberately draws attention to its autobiographical basis. Stead is again casting her narrative line into the waters of her own youthful experience. But now, with *The Man Who Loved Children* behind her, she is able finally to make use of materials she had drafted as long ago as the early 1930s in Paris.

These included several schemes for a series of stories following the stages of a woman's life, and pages of erotic sketches and lists. She had also worked on pieces entitled 'The Young Man will Go Far' and 'The Wraith and the Wanderer', some of which went into *The Beauties and Furies* (1936). Such evidence of earlier attempts to deal with the Jonathan Crow figure might suggest that it was only when she had worked out a way of using this kind of autobiographical material in her fiction, that she was ready, well on in her publishing career, to complete the story. It was perhaps the emotional account-settling with the figure of her father in the previous novel which enabled Stead now to put the young woman at centre stage as the single protagonist.[3]

The material of *For Love Alone* is more directly autobiographical than that of its predecessor. Like Teresa Hawkins, Christina Stead spent her early twenties in Sydney working in an ill-paid office job instead of the teaching for which she had been trained, starving herself of sustenance of all kinds so as to save the fare for her passage to Europe. She too, having finally reached London and the man she had decided years before was the one for her, instead fell in love and went to live with an American who was to be her life partner from then on. These events provide the plot line of the novel. The Sydney setting—the family home at Watson's Bay (Fisherman's Bay in the novel), the city and the university—is left unchanged, though the autobiographical material is transposed in time, as it is in *The Man Who Loved Children*, to take place in the 1930s.

As with the previous novel, the autobiographical reading which is 'authorized' by Stead in interviews sets strict limits to interpretation. She insisted that Teresa's struggle is not for independence but 'to achieve union with a man, that's what it is':[4] and she rejected all such terms as 'liberation', 'escape' and 'expatriate artist', claiming that it was not so much dissatisfaction with her lot that motivates Teresa as 'the impulse of the young to wander'. It seems clear that she was, in these comments, rejecting two cultural myths that have frequently been invoked in readings of *For Love Alone*: that of the necessary self-exile of the artist from 'his' provincial home (a particularly potent myth in Australian literary culture),[5] and that of the necessary independence from men of the feminist heroine (a myth popular in the 1970s with male and female critics alike).[6]

While these objections on the writer's part can be seen as merely a rather cranky resistance to labels of any kind, they do in fact point to two emphases in the novel that belie both its autobiographical origin and the implications of its title. She is pointing to the fact that it is not a romantic Joycean myth of the artist, despite Teresa's 'being' herself and beginning to write. However it is romantic in the rather archaic sense of the heroic and idealistic quest for love: Teresa like any feminist heroine is determined to break out of the social mould set for her life, to seek out her own grandly conceived 'destiny', but central to that impulse, and to the concerns of the story, is her sexuality and her desire actively to know love. What's more, the novel does not disabuse her of the expectation that she can get for herself 'love, learning, bread', the three things she wants, although in order to get them she has to run the gauntlet of misogynist ideologies and practices in her relationship with Jonathan Crow (who is not only a 'one-horse pedant', as James Quick calls him (p.416), but a one-horse misogynist). How the novel comes to arrive at such a romantic, even utopian, outcome is an important and intriguing question for any feminist reader to confront. Yet such a reading must also take account of the deeply ironic possibilities of the title, of a heroine named after St Teresa of Avila, and of the epigraph from *Don Quixote*, an exchange between two horses about the nature of love, which concludes: 'you grow metaphysical' (response) 'From lack of food'.[7]

The doubly heroic associations of an *epic* journey into life and a *quest* for love as its meaning are evoked in the novel's prologue, 'Sea People'. It is a prose poem which gives a positive twist to the colonial-expatriate myth by characterizing Australia, the 'island continent in the water hemisphere', as a locus of legend as rich as the Old World (which is later celebrated in a matching virtuoso piece as 'the land of ice-Cockaigne'; p.189). Here the European inhabitants appear as born wanderers over the seas of the world ('each Australian is a Ulysses', declares Teresa later, p.222):

> It is a fruitful island of the sea-world, a great Ithaca, there parched and stony and here trodden by flocks and curly-headed bulls and heavy with thick-set grain. To this race can be put the famous question: 'Oh, Australian, have you just come from the harbour? Is your ship in the roadstead? Men of what nation put you down—for I am sure you did not get here on foot?' (p. 2)

The distinction between legend and social reality which is one of the major axes of the narrative is not located in opposing places, the Old and the New Worlds, but rather in two dimensions of the heroine's experience, her mental life of fantasy and speculation and her relations with other people and their constructions of reality. The gap between the two dimensions, a space traditionally for the play of irony, is where will and knowledge operate—the arena of the *Bildung*.

Despite the intense isolation and self-centredness of Teresa, and the steady narrative focus on her, Stead manages to evoke the social presence of cities and people around her. By choosing to set the events of the novel

almost a decade later than her own departure from
Sydney in 1928, she makes Teresa's harsh regimen of
saving and starving coincide with the worst years of the
Depression in Sydney. Details of the period confirm her
sense of entrapment in senseless and punitive social
forms, for instance an official requirement that women
teachers who marry must resign from the state
education service. Other such details include a lock-out
at the factory where her brother, Leo, works, and the
dumping of unsold produce in the harbour near their
home while her relatives go bankrupt on their orchard
block. Teresa's cousins' 'marriage-fever', her retarded
pupils' disabilities, her fellow students' dissatisfactions,
all function to express this material and spiritual
impoverishment and hunger. Even the ideas about
sexual and economic oppression introduced by Jonathan
Crow articulate a pessimistic determinism, rather than
celebrating the Bohemian alternatives that might have
been encountered in the 1920s by Stead herself.[8]

Also lacking from the Sydney scene is any representation of the kinds of political engagement that might
have captured the imagination of students, at least, in
the early 1920s. Such radical political and sexual
possibilities only enter the space of the novel with the
advent of James Quick and his cosmopolitan friends in
London—for it is a major part of his function to make the
world come alive for Teresa, as she tells him (p. 390). For
the most part, however, Crow's theories of social
determinism serve to underline the sharp separation
between Teresa's fantasies of freedom and love, and
possible social realities. In this novel, the realist details of
the Depression years are subordinated to, and expressive of, the urgency of the protagonist's desires. The
focus is on the individual, not the collectivity (as it was in
the earlier *Seven Poor Men of Sydney*), and on the personal
quest rather than the social realities of the early 1930s.[9]

In this protagonist-centred narrative, much of the action goes on in her imagination, or in the talk she listens to, or it is presented as the projection of her imagination into the natural and social world (for instance, the feverish excitement of 'Malfi's Wedding', or the sexual 'battlefield' that she senses around her as she walks home in the dark afterwards). Such constant activity of thought and imagination prompted one critic, refuting claims that the novel was shapeless, to characterize it as a 'meditation on love'.[10] A meditation is, of course, the formal structure suggested by Teresa's composition, after the manner of her saintly namesake, entitled 'The Seven Houses of Love'. It is not hard to find parallels in her story with these 'houses' or stations: Pastorale, Bacchanale, Klingsor's Garden ('yearning lust'), the alternating houses of Creation and Imagination, the identical houses of Heaven and Hell ('relation with a single human being') and the last house, Extinction ('to die terribly by will') (pp. 419-21).

Yet the novel creates a multitude of meanings around love/sex/destiny, not only through Teresa's differing experiences of fantasy and relationship, but also through the variety of discourses on those subjects that make up its heterogeneous texture. It is, like all of Stead's, a polyphonic novel of the kind Bakhtin attributes to Dostoyevsky (one of Stead's most admired novelists). In the polyphonic novel there is no single discourse and no hierarchy of discourses established by a unified narrative consciousness. There is always a mixture of discourses, but its constitution changes throughout.[11] In most of Stead's writing, each character's way of speaking is identifiable with a known social discourse rather than appearing to be the effusions of a unique personality.

The novel's early sections are dominated by Teresa's erotic daydreams, furnished by her searches through the literature and art of the past, in tension with all the popular wisdom about marriage picked up from cousins and friends, mixed with strains of her father's lofty Victorian sentiments on sexual beauty, harmony and freedom. Into this mêlée Jonathan Crow introduces a heavy dose of hard-headed Darwinian theorizing on sex and survival (biological and social), and builds on it as the narrative proceeds with a wealth of popularized psychology of the racist and sexist kind predominant in the inter-war years. This discourse almost wins out, as we see in Teresa's despairing decision to 'die by will' because Jonathan has rejected her: accepting his verdict that she has failed in her biological destiny as a woman, she tells herself, 'So much the worse for you, says nature. So much the worse for the woman who can't get a man. I don't care, says nature, die, then' (p. 346). But at this point in the narrative she is 'rescued', and the literary discourses that have always sustained her are supplemented by James Quick's crash course in erotic poetry and obscene limericks, and given a new context of revolutionary political ideas. The evocation of traditional romance, where the woman is not the questor but its object, is prominent in the novel's complex resolution— and something of an embarrassment for feminist readings.

Symphonic Structure

A way of describing the powerful and complex orchestration of journey structure, narrational stance and textual heterogeneity is suggested by a chance remark made by Christina Stead in an interview, that she thought of the structure of her novels as 'symphonic'.[12] The classic symphony is a sonata for full orchestra, developing two major themes with contrasting rhythms through four movements, in which pace and textual density vary. A reading of the novel as analogous to this musical form can enable us to specify the political and textual complexities offered by this narrative of a woman's quest for love.

The first of the novel's four movements carries it as far as the failure of Teresa's journey to Harper's Ferry (Chapter 14). Following the opening scene with the father (which I have discussed earlier), the chapters divide into two groups dealing with the outer life of social reality (family, the wedding, school and friends, the 'iron circle of home and work', p. 85) around an intervening section on Teresa's inner life, which is distinguished by exalted, allusive language, excited rhythms and obscure incidents. In the three chapters concerning her flight to Narara, the two dimensions of inner and outer life are brought into close conjunction as her fantasy of escape attains the status of an expedition. The expedition fails in its practical object, but that is barely noticeable as the scene takes on Biblical resonances. Teresa wanders all day in circles around the valley ('great, fruitful, silent as paradise', p. 163) with Biblical phrases echoing in her head. Pursued along the track by a leering old man waving his penis at her, she thinks of Noah's daughters: 'they were punished who uncovered their father's nakedness. Why would an old man publish his own shame?' (p. 166). None of this is resolved in her conscious mind—indeed, all she comes home with (ignominiously fetched by brother Lance) is the conviction that she will give up teaching and will never marry the boy next door, like her cousin. Yet some unconscious resolution is signalled in the moment she decides to turn back: 'a deep melancholy came over her at the sight and smell of the great valley with all its slopes far and untrodden by her. She loved it. What a hidden life it had' (p. 166). Despite suggestions of the snake in the Garden of Eden it is not so much a knowledge of good and evil that she gains, as an acceptance of the female body evoked by this image of the valley. Her earlier vision of Harper's Ferry was, in contrast to this, 'a lonely, dark, dread, endlessly solitary, inhuman place . . . a drear wild crossing' (p. 139).

In the second movement, which concludes with her departure for London in pursuit of Jonathan, the twin themes of imprisonment and flight that were established in the first movement are taken up again in something like a minor key. It is now her isolation that becomes imprisoning, for her anguish at the 'extreme deed' she has committed in declaring herself to Jonathan has left her with no confidantes. The narrator comments: 'The deeds of the moral inventor are always criminal and their most evil effect is that when done secretly they cut the doer off from society; put around, they attract adherents' (p. 226). Also, with a change of scene to the university milieu, the rest of the social world falls away. Talk dominates, and after Jonathan's departure this narrows down to Teresa's inner monologues as she walks to and from her job. With these compulsive repetitions of talking and walking, the orchestration is less rich and varied, with a more cerebral concentration on the operations of will and determination. The climax of the movement is marked, again, by an expedition, another failed one, when Teresa, having starved herself for three years and in a state of nervous collapse, attempts to sleep out overnight in the vacant lot behind the factory, in order to save more money. As before, this practical goal, and her conviction afterwards that she will not submit to the seductive attentions of her workmate, Erskine, seem beside the point. Again, her confusion is resolved not by rational understanding but by a simple, inexplicable turning away (literally) from her plan. Hidden in the vacant lot, she sees a man come in and relieve himself by the fence:

> In her ignorance of men's ways, she supposed this man was like the man on the road long ago at Narara, and she became very much afraid. She rose, trembling—what excuse could she give if she was seen coming out of the lot at this time of night? She came out boldly; so much the worse, she would explain that she had to fix her stockings.... She began to walk down her old route, heel and toe, heel and toe, in the old strong rhythm, carrying her valise. (p. 287)

The hallucinatory quality of the scene, like the paradisical valley scene, recalls the wandering tales section of the *Odyssey*, a heroic journey which Teresa is to evoke yet again, in the next movement, when her self-imprisonment appears to have become complete and she chides herself for her 'buffoon odyssey'.

Beginning with Part 2 of the novel, and Teresa's arrival in London, the third movement picks up speed, but with a sickening see-saw rhythm as it measures her exchanges with Jonathan. The atmosphere of entrapment and emotional enclosure is intensified as the writing swings back and forth between Jonathan's theories and tales of his sufferings and his friends' sexual exploits, and Teresa's secret searching for the clue to their 'eternal maddening conversation' and her periodic attempts to break away. It is relieved only by the occasional presence of James Quick, Teresa's employer, who is represented not only through his talk but also through his wanderings in the streets of London, where he is a stranger as well. In this movement there are several shifts of narrative perspective away from Teresa and onto Crow or Quick. Its finale takes place in an appropriately dark setting, a deserted sawmill in which Teresa and Jonathan have taken shelter during one of their country walks. The sudden rainstorm sets the mill-wheel in violent motion: 'Grinding and groaning, shrieking, it turned downwards into the boiling pool while the timbers tried to rear part' (p. 407). Across the gaping hole in the mill floor,

> They looked at each other by the light of the flare with unveiled dislike. Teresa, looking at him, released him from her will; it happened suddenly. The harness of years dropped off, eaten through; she dropped her eyes, thought: 'How stupid he is! How dull!' (p. 408)

It is the decisive moment of release but, again, not a rational decision; nor is she concerned to follow through with her perception of his stupidity and dullness, despite Quick's eagerness to demonstrate this to her. The simple statement, 'She released him from her will', signals the final playing out of the Nietzschean belief that 'Willing emancipateth', which they have both held, but so differently.[13]

The beginning of the fourth and final movement promises resolution as it clarifies much of what has gone before through Quick's response to two bizarre documents, Jonathan's essay on the inferiority of women, and Teresa's 'Seven Houses of Love', subtitled 'A system by which the Chaste can Know Love'. But with the flowering of the Teresa–Quick relationship, a new double movement begins. A rapid succession of discoveries, sexual and intellectual, is punctuated by moments in which Teresa has to take account of her lover's difference from herself, and of the fact that he loves her in return. She fears that the 'night of the senses' that she has dreamed of will trap her in the 'marriage sleep' that is the usual end of the woman's love story (p. 463). Now that her desires are accepted and loved, she wants to go further, to try out her power with men (p. 464). This conflict is played out in her affair with Harry Girton, and it is their semi-clandestine meeting in Oxford that provides the occasion for this movement's visionary climax. The chapter title from Donne's 'Epithalamium', 'Today put on perfection (and a woman's name)', names *this* incident as her wedding—though not to the man to whom she will return, Quick. Again, the restlessness of desire is imaged in walking, and kinaesthetic imagery is continued in the moment when, alone, she feels 'something of the first feeling of all':

> Down below flowed a great slaty river, smooth but covered with twisted threads of water, swollen with its great flow, and directly under the window was an immense dusk-white flower with drooping petals, surrounded by green and living leaves....'Time is already floating away,' she thought, smiling peculiarly. She was astonished at her feeling of wanting nothing. (pp.489-90)

This mythical moment is followed by two further finales, as in many symphonies: one for full orchestra, whom she will return, Quick. Again, the restlessness of the 'citied plain' of human history, and a coda, in which she catches sight of Crow in the street and concludes with the question that revives the whole paradox of desire is imaged in walking, and kinaesthetic imagery is repeated forever, he—and me! What's there to stop it?' (p. 502).

'A young woman's entrance into the world': Feminist Genre Criticism

To read this novel as belonging to the genre of personal quest is inevitably to link it with many others by twentieth-century women writers—for instance, Doris Lessing's Martha Quest novels and *The Golden Notebook*. It is also to enter into a well-developed discussion among feminist critics on women's interventions into this genre, the novel of development or of existential quest. I want to look at some examples of this criticism, both for its specific relevance to *For Love Alone* and as an example of what genre criticism has to offer. Broadly defined, considerations of genre raise questions about the kinds of plot, the types of protagonist, the narrative stances and discursive registers that were available to women writers at a given time, and about the uses they made of these devices. Genre has always been gendered, fiction being considered suitable for women to attempt, but not poetry and drama. Within the house of fiction, plots are strictly gendered, as indicated by the gradual elision between 'romance' and 'love story' in the late nineteenth century, and the consignment of the masculine romance under the general name of 'adventure story'.[14] Feminist genre criticism attends to women writers' adaptations (sometimes subversions) of gendered literary genres. As well, the area of genre and gender accommodates questions about the material determinants of these generic codes, their changes over time, and the social conditions of their accessibility to women.

Within feminist criticism there has been much interest in the novel of development, the *Bildungsroman*, as a genre popular with women writers since the early nineteenth century. Feminist critics re-examining definitions of the genre from a gendered perspective in *The Voyage In: Fictions of Female Development* identify 'distinctively female versions of the *Bildungsroman*'. These are described in terms of recurrent narrative structures (the apprenticeship and the awakening) and recurrent thematic tensions 'between autonomy and relationship, separation and community, loyalty to women and attraction to men'.[15] The editors claim that these are specifically female tensions, and while conceding that social constraints produce other conflicts that are not unique to women, they claim that these conflicts are more relentless in women's stories:

> Repeatedly, the female protagonist or *Bildungsheld* must chart a treacherous course between the penalties of expressing sexuality and suppressing it, between the costs of inner concentration and of direct confrontation with society, between the price of succumbing to madness and of grasping a repressive 'normality'.[16]

This would suggest that *For Love Alone* is unusual among women's novels in that Teresa always is quite clear about choosing the anti-social side of each one of these dilemmas. Believing in principle in the expression of sexuality, she scorns conventional female prudery and timidity; but she is susceptible to Jonathan Crow precisely because he talks sex and practises a perverse chastity. Her few direct confrontations with social convention are confusing to others and humiliating to her, such as her refusal to dive for the bridal bouquet at Malfi's wedding and her running away from teaching — but in each case the vivid reality of her fantasy life sustains her conviction that she is doing the right thing. Despite her earlier fear of the madness that she believed to be attendant on sexual repression, she welcomes the willed madness of her isolated dedication to following Jonathan: 'it seemed proof that she was very strange indeed—and to strange persons, strange visions, strange destinies' (p. 265). But finally, having followed the logic of that 'inner concentration' almost to the brink of suicide, Teresa re-emerges, still demanding 'love, knowledge, bread—all these I will have', and seizes what she wants—a committed partnership with a man (but not marriage and suburbia), knowledge of the world, and her own creative work. Triumphant but not free of conflict, she can be read as a twentieth-century sexual rebel who succeeds.

This is, of course, why it is tempting to read *For Love Alone* as a manifesto of sexual liberation, if not of feminism. But the story it tells of 'a young girl's entrance into the world' does not match the pattern of the female *Bildungsroman* traced by the editors of *The Voyage In*. To point this out is not to cast doubt on the value of genre definitions *per se*, but rather to test the outer limits of this currently influential feminist account of the novel of development. My reading of Stead's novel questions this structural model by pointing to its dependence on a psychological theory of individual development and sexual difference, one which deflects attention from the heterogeneity of writing and which is not well equipped to discern the concepts of social structure and change that are deployed in particular fictions.

While the editors of *The Voyage In* readily concede that the balance of tensions within the genre shifts with history, and note in twentieth-century fictions of female development 'a movement from the world within to the world without, from introspection to activity',[17] it seems inadequate simply to gesture towards 'history' itself as the determinant of changing structures. It is as if the differences between *For Love Alone* and Woolf's *The Voyage Out* (a paradigm case for the book's thesis, echoed in its title) could be explained by women's greater access to freedom of movement during the period between the two world wars. Teresa's voyage is equally mental and physical, and what enables her to grasp both independence and love is not so much a changed social world as a different vision of its dynamics and possibilities. Social and personal freedom such as she finds are one possibility, but so too is further entanglement in the 'difficult social web' (p. 254) that is spun to contain human passions.

In all of Stead's fiction, conflict is imaged in hand-to-hand combat between lovers or family members.

Compared with the pattern in Woolf's *The Voyage Out* of the individual young woman ranged against overwhelming social and metaphysical forces, Stead constructs a fictional world in which those forces are internalized by the characters and become forces in their own mental life, enacted in the clash of wills in a violent struggle for psychic survival. It is psychology in this sense, as internalized social forces at war within and between persons, that is implied by Stead's self-description as a writer of 'the psychological drama of the person'. This vision of personal conflict and social-historical dynamics enables her to portray 'the young woman's entrance into the world' as ultimately the triumph of the social rebel.

Such a vision is incompatible with the concepts of psychology and social dynamics that are implicit in the feminist criticism represented by the essays in *The Voyage In*. By and large they share the mother-centred psychological theory of sexual difference which we encountered in the previous chapter. The editors quote Nancy Chodorow on sexual difference: 'The basic feminine sense of self is connected to the world, the basic masculine sense of self is separate';[18] the implication is that fictions tracing this development of self will be *essentially* different for women and for men. And so it is proposed, following Carole Gilligan's theory of the different moral development of women and men, that 'A distinctive female "I" implies a distinctive value system and unorthodox developmental goals, defined in terms of community and empathy rather than achievement and autonomy.'[19] The problem with this claim, as with the psychological essentialism proposed by Chodorow, is that it confirms rather than deconstructs the male/autonomy, female/community opposition—a deconstruction that is crucially necessary in order to reveal the dependence of the one (the male side of the opposition) on the suppression of the other. What is cause for concern here is the dominance in U S feminism of a theory of sexual difference that does not directly contest the way phallocentrism constitutes itself upon that culturally constructed difference.

In this structuralist phase in feminist criticism, such a theory of psychological structure is held to underlie and be reflected in common or recurrent literary structures. Thus the 'deep structure' of the women's novel of development or quest is often held to be the loss and redemption of the mother–daughter bond as the psychic economy upon which a woman must develop her autonomous sense of self. Several interesting essays on the twentieth-century female *Kunstlerroman*, the novel of the artist's development, demonstrate the working of this structuralist assumption in relation to that sub-group of *Bildungsromane* to which both *The Man Who Loved Children* and *For Love Alone* could be said to belong. Susan Gubar, finding in the work of Woolf, Mansfield and other modernists an exploration of 'the mother–daughter bond as a release from the solipsism of individual consciousness', lists three shifts in perspective that allowed them to reshape the structure:

> [F]irst, domestic disease or sickness *of* home is imaginatively reconstructed as sickness *for* home in what amounts to a revisionary domestic mythology; second, silent female resistance to or retaliation against the male word transforms itself into fantasies of a woman's language; finally, matrophobia, fear of becoming the mother, turns into matrisexuality, the erotics of mother and child.[20]

But, she says, this modernist-feminist assertion of a 'natural and distinct sphere' fell victim to its conservative consequences, and by the time *The Man Who Loved Children* appears, the utopian project of women's *Kunstlerromane* is all but extinguished 'when the daughter-artist can only respond to her mother's painful cry, "My womb is tearing" with the act of matricide'.[21]

Rachel Blau DuPlessis identifies the two elements in tension in the female novel of development as the love plot and the *Bildungs* plot, and points out the way this tension is exacerbated in the figure of the female artist. In most nineteenth-century female artist novels, the tension is resolved by the triumph of the love plot: formation or development ends, and social integration happens through marriage or not at all—the heroine dies or goes mad. The pattern she finds in some twentieth-century female artist fictions, however, overcomes this split by redefining both love and art: 'The romance plot, which often turns into a stalemate, is displaced ... and replaced by a triangular plot of nurturance offered to an emergent daughter by a parental couple.'[22] Most often, the mother becomes the muse, and the daughter's task is to complete the mother's work:

> This intellectual, aesthetic and ethical defense of the mother becomes involved with the evocation of the preoedipal dyad, matrisexuality, or a bisexual oscillation deep in the gendering process. In these works, the female artist is given a way of looping back and re-enacting childhood ties, to achieve not the culturally-approved ending in heterosexual romance, but rather the re-parenting necessary to her second birth as an artist.[23]

Following Judith Kegan Gardiner, she cites *The Man Who Loved Children* as an example of maternal death as a 'necessary enabling act, which distinguishes the useful from the damaging in the maternal heritage'.[24] Now, while that novel could be read in terms of this proposed triangular plot (which, perversely, nurtures Louie's talent by setting it huge obstacles to overcome), it is

certainly not the case that *For Love Alone* could be read as
displacing the heterosexual romance plot. Stead rede-
fines love and marriage, instead of refusing them or
even 'working through' them, as Lessing does in *The
Golden Notebook*. *For Love Alone* begins with the symbolic
death of the father and establishes the emotional logic of
what is to follow: in Teresa's libidinal economy, the
sadistic man, in the mould of her father, is the more
powerful attraction, despite her fantasy of love as
freedom. If she could succeed in loving Jonathan she
would redeem the 'murder' of Andrew Hawkins. He, like
the father, invites women to 'do the work of passion' for
him, a self-confessed 'gadfly of desire' who likes to
observe 'scientifically' women's arousal. By denying his
own desire and witholding consummation, he embodies
that cultural presence of the Father which was discussed
in the previous chapter—the denial, the illegitimation, of
female desire. Thus he represents the stalemate of
heterosexual romance, which Teresa herself breaks
with the help of a nurturing male lover. Furthermore,
Stead destabilizes this second love-plot by Teresa's
insistence on trying out her power over men while
remaining loyal to Quick as 'the only love, but not the
first and not the last' (p.496).

DuPlessis claims, too, that the art work represented in
these female *Kunstlerromane* 'has a poetics of domestic
values—nurturance, community building, inclu-
siveness, empathetic care' and because these poetics
begin with its ethics, not its aesthetics, 'it is very like
"life"'.[25] Yet this is manifestly not the case with either
Louie's play or with Teresa's 'The Seven Houses of
Love'. On the contrary, what strikes one is their
profound literariness, and their bringing into play the
unresolved conflicts of mental life through the working
of fantasy. Teresa's writing, like her namesake saint's
visionary work, *The Interior Castle*, articulates the desire

for an impossible union. In each, too, desire is struggle as well as ecstasy and the beloved turns out to be also an adversary (Jonathan Crow's initials suggest this aspect of his role in Teresa's quest). Her description of the work, the completion of which will be her death, is *perversely* nurturing, empathetic: 'these pale leaves of poor sterile women, floated off the tree of flesh, would not have been without someone to carry their words, ... would, dead, dying and to come, have an advocate in the courts of the world' (pp.419–20).

The point is not that *For Love Alone* is unique, nor that it is deviant from this preferred model in feminist criticism, but that the model is too limited. It tends to set up a literary and psychological norm of femininity; and if, instead of a male model of the *Bildungsroman* that endorses patriarchal values, we now have an established feminist model of psychic and artistic development based on a notion of essential femininity, then we have no more than an inversion of the original patriarchal structure. Secondly, the specific problem posed for feminist readings of *For Love Alone* by this kind of structuralist criticism is how to accommodate both the romance genre (the 'for love alone' element) and the quest or *Bildungsroman* or *Kunstlerroman* (for autonomy, identity, creativity).

A Quest for Love

As we have seen, it is far from inevitable that the love-story plot disappears, although some feminist critics tend to wish it away, to insist that although Teresa thinks she is seeking a man's love, she is 'really looking for herself'.[26] It is as if a serious novel about a woman can no longer be a love-story. Yet it is crucial to recognize that the terms of Teresa's quest are about the *world* rather than the self—about the finding or making of a place, a person or persons, from which to know the world, to create its meanings. If anything, it is a *Bildungsroman* of the kind that Bakhtin wrote about as one where not only the protagonist but the world itself was in process of change, and where the protagonist 'is forced to become a new, unprecedented type of human being' because the *foundations* of the world are changing. In such a novel of emergence, 'problems of reality and man's (sic) potential, problems of freedom and necessity, and the problem of creative initiative' are crucial, and the human image 'enters into a completely new, *spatial* sphere of historical existence'.[27] It is this aspect of the novel that achieves completion in the image of Teresa's emergence from the 'womb of time' into the 'cited plain' of history. Her joining with the liberated masses may be read as a utopian resolution to the story of women, men and love, but one which incorporates struggle and change.

Where Stead is most radical in this female *Bildungsroman* is her transformation of the oppositional thematics of love and independence by vindicating Teresa's idealistic quest for both. Her dedication to 'love alone' is portrayed as dedication to a principle, not a person—to a dynamic principle of Eros, of creative struggle. It is love conceived of as a passion, a kind of knowledge and a kind of power. It links the saint with the sensualist, the individual with the collective history, the human and the natural worlds.

A measure of the transformation performed in Stead's novel can be gained by comparing it with George Eliot's *Middlemarch*, where St Theresa is also invoked as the prototype of the woman questor. Where Eliot's 'Prelude' refers to those 'later-born Theresas' of her time whose ardour 'alternated between a vague ideal and the common yearning of womanhood', Stead's Teresa fuses together in her passion the ideal and the yearning. It is passion which, with her, 'performs the function of knowledge for the ardently willing soul', in Eliot's words. It was Eliot's view that this function could only be performed by a 'coherent social faith and order' such as that which had enabled the original Theresa to realize her ideal of 'an epic life wherein there was a constant unfolding of far-resonant action', but this seemed no longer possible.[28] Eliot's Dorothea turns to secular love as the means of realizing her aspirations, and to a particular man as her guide to knowledge, like many nineteenth-century heroines.[29] The *Middlemarch* pattern, where the unloving scholar is superseded by the loving man of the world, is repeated in *For Love Alone*, but here the heroine need not resign herself to a conventional marriage, to living vicariously through her husband an obscure life of 'incalculably diffusive' beneficial effects. There is no 'coherent social faith and order', nor even the promise of a new one, like that held out by Will Ladislaw in *Middlemarch*. Yet there is the principle of love as creative struggle which Teresa defends and demonstrates: having taken on the position of social rebel, she continues the experiment of living her life against the grain of the dominant culture.[30]

A solution to the problem of what status to afford the love story has been offered by feminist and other critics' accounts of the operation of irony in Stead's narrative. Stead certainly entertains the possibility of Teresa's quest for love being read ironically: she has Quick declare that her devotion to Jonathan was 'just the illusion of a love-hungry girl' and Teresa agrees that she 'can't believe I ever loved that man' (p.502). In this light, the pattern is banal: first she picks Mr Wrong because she is only an idealistic and inexperienced girl, and then she is rewarded by the appearance of Mr Right. But Mr Right has no monopoly on wisdom, and the relationship with him is deliberately destabilized by the encounter with Girton (Teresa's college education, perhaps?). An ironic reading may point to the truism that 'self-deception awaits the idealist',[31] that is, the expression of desire in fantasy and speculation is bound to go wrong and, indeed, that being 'undeceived' and wise to the ways of the world is unquestionably first priority. Yet the very presence of Jonathan Crow's constant lectures on self-interest and the survival of the psychologically fittest is enough to cast a shadow on this reading of the novel; and then there is Teresa's declaration, *'Love is blind* is the dictum, whereas, with me at least, Love sees everything. Like insanity, it sees everything; like insanity, it must not reveal its thoughts' (p.460).

I would argue, rather, that criticism based on a moral reading of classic nineteenth-century realism *expects* a fictional protagonist to move from innocence to experience, and expects to be assigned by the narrative a superior position of knowledge from which to perceive this progress. Such expectations become banal in the case of the female novel of development because we 'know' that a girl's high expectations of love and autonomy are bound to be disappointed (whether this knowledge is accompanied by 'realistic' patriarchal regret or 'romantic' feminist anger). The move from innocence to experience is not the same thing for a young woman as for a young man. The outcome is likely to be tragic (like Hardy's heroines) or a noble accommodation to a limited sphere (like James's young women) rather than a 'realistic' finding of one's place in the world, a proper and constructive tempering of 'great expectations'.

As a feminist critic sensitive to this difference, Lidoff develops an ironic reading which relegates the 'romance' element of the heroine's quest to the realm of the inner life and classifies the narrator's stance as that of a 'realism' which allows both sympathetic identification and ironic distance.[32] However, I would argue that it is time to drop the dichotomy between realism and romance defined as moral attitudes, and the notion of irony that is its corollary. It is a limiting one for feminist criticism to be stuck with, and particularly so in relation to Stead's tales of women's lives, for they inscribe ideologies of femininity that cannot be definitively assigned to either side of the dichotomy. On this question of the status of love and ideas about love in the novel, Jennifer Strauss suggests that Stead seems to be demonstrating that 'the confusions concerning love, lust and marriage are real confusions, cases not of mere mistaken identity, but of identities overlapping and intertwining'.[33] And Teresa's ideas are inevitably like a wardrobe of hand-me-downs where nothing fits exactly but everything has some usefulness or some attraction. The patriarchal cultural inheritance of a young woman, even if she is trying to 'make over' conventional expectations that she find her place and value in marriage by the creative addition of erotic literature, Nietzschean metaphysics, nineteenth-century social theory, and so on, is bound to fall short of her needs and expectations:

> Teresa knew all the disorderly loves of Ovid, the cruel luxury of Petronius, the exorbitance of Aretino, the meaning of the witches' Sabbaths, the experiments of Sade, the unimaginable horrors of the Inquisition, the bestiality of the Bible, the bitter jokes of Aristophanes and what the sex-psychologists had written.... [T]he poets and play-wrights spoke the language she knew, and the satirists and moralists wrote down with stern and marvellous precision all that she knew in herself but kept hidden from family and friends. (p.76)

Teresa apprentices herself to this philosophy of passion rather as the classic nineteenth-century male *Bildungsheld* was indentured to a philosophy of life. Classically, this hero develops from innocence to knowledge through an exposure to experience that tempers his idealism. The major difference here is that the young woman forges the philosophy herself, out of her fantasies and the scraps of knowledge that she manages to glean from reading and talking.

It is, of course, tested by experience, but not in the banal sense of disillusionment or correction. In her meditations on passion and social mores, she concludes that women must always have desired as she does, but never uttered their desire, not acted upon it (p.101). Timidity seems to her women's great weakness, and she resolves to act as (she believes) no woman has ever done, in defiance of man-made laws to control passion (p.93). That her action takes the form of a declaration of love to a frigid misogynist, Jonathan Crow, is an irony with as much comic as tragic potential. Yet however romantically conceived, this 'extreme deed' proves to be the action which makes everything else possible, thus vindicating the seriousness with which this idealist takes her ideas.

Such a reading of the *productive* force of frustrated desires could be applied to all of Stead's fiction, from the heroic *For Love Alone* to the satirical portraits and the deeply ironic later novels. Ideas and fantasies have a material force in the lives of all her characters, whether dangerous or beneficent, and are not conducive to correction and control, as they are in liberal humanism. Characters change direction because of their instincts for psychic survival or destruction, not because of reconsidering their ideas. Stead's construction of 'character' in this way involves a certain deployment of irony, but one that differs from the humanist ideas of classic realism, and which can coexist with a utopian degree of idealism—as *For Love Alone* demonstrates.

Chapter Four

Two Portraits: *Letty Fox* and *Miss Herbert*

Two conflicting visions haunt the ending of *For Love Alone:* the circles of desire and domination 'going on for ever' between women and men, and the young woman's entry into human history, imaged as a march across the 'citied plain'. The story of the 'free woman' which might have followed from this historic moment never appeared among Stead's fictions. Teresa is the only heroic figure among her lives of modern women. Next, then, I want to consider two ironic, even satirical, portraits of modern women struggling alone in the city, preeminently creatures of their time and place but also rootless, alienated and without faith in either love or destiny. *Letty Fox: Her Luck* (1946) and *Miss Herbert (The Suburban Wife)* (1976), although published thirty years apart, were written at about the same time in the late 1940s and early 1950s. Both novels are more readily imaged in the circlings of frustrated will and desire than in the outward flight or the onward march of the 'free woman'. Like painted portraits they guide the eye in concentric circles, and each is characterized by a rhythm of repetition rather than a strong narrative line.

Anti-Heroines

The narrative, always in close-up, accumulates details without ever clarifying direction. The concluding words of each protagonist reiterate this sense of aimless movement:

> ...but I'm no tea leaf reader. I can only tangle with situations as they come along. *On s'engage et puis on voit. (Letty Fox)*[1]

> 'I kept to the rules, but the rules didn't keep me. But I hewed to the line; I cultivated my garden.' *(Miss Herbert)*[2]

Each of these heroines emphasizes both her anti-heroism and her struggle for self-respect. In this way they sign themselves as pre-eminently bourgeois figures, portraits of middle-class women (North American and English, respectively) who proudly proclaim their own ordinariness: 'just an ordinary woman' (Eleanor), a 'typical New York girl' (Letty). It is a mark of the peculiarity of Stead's ironic portraits that this claim is presented as part of their strength, their robust gift for social conformity and thus survival, even while their capacity to deny responsibility for their actions by hiding behind that same claim to ordinariness is being exposed by the narrative's ironies. Letty, claiming always to shrink from 'what was beyond the pale' (p. 4), is portrayed as a female adept of the sexual picaresque; Eleanor, the ladylike English rose, is observed engaging in all manner of sexual and social hypocrisies.

Yet neither novel could be satisfactorily described as a study in bad faith, for the portraitist's ironic shading moves sometimes into the sharp contrasts of satire, sometimes in the opposite direction towards straight reportage. Because of this variation, the position constructed for the reader to occupy proves unstable, and there is no easy access to either judgement or sympathetic identification of the kind one expects as a reader of realist narrative. The instability of one's position as reader is the more noticeable because both are *single* portraits, concentrating fully on the female protagonist (even more than on Teresa in *For Love Alone*), so that other characters are known only through their report, or in relation to them.

That is to say, these single portraits are presented as self-portraits. Letty tells her story in her own words, while Eleanor's is reported from her own purblind point of view, with her own line in clichés. Each woman is made up out of her language, which is itself made up out of the discourses of contemporary capitalist popular culture—populist political rhetoric, women's magazine advice columns, and so on. But both, too, are educated women, and just as likely as Louie or Teresa to appropriate for themselves the commonplaces of European high culture. The situations in which they do so, however, render such allusions ironic, if not satirical: Letty's Napoleonic motto *('on s'engage et puis on voit')* sees her through some particularly fierce and sordid campaigns in the sex war, while Eleanor Herbert ('I cultivated my garden') emerges as a female Candide whose innocence is dangerous indeed. Yet the ironic presentation of these women is not entirely at their expense, for it shows them struggling to construct their own subjectivities out of the ideological materials at hand. It is a technique involving fidelity to these materials, and implying an unusual respect for the ways in which they function as structures of reality, as truths, for these social/historical subjects. Its targets are social and political rather than personal and moral.

If we read these novels to learn 'what women have felt and experienced',[3] then we shall only learn again what misogynists have always maintained, that women are innately conservative—for this is how they present themselves. These somewhat disreputable protagonists seem far from providing the kind of access to female experience which has been most prized in feminist literary criticism. Neither heroines nor victims of patriarchal society, each is thoroughly a creature of her time, as she is formed by, and engages in articulating, the ideologies and institutions of her particular society. They portray women living out the realities of these ideologies, and yet each 'lives a full life, she fulfils herself in her own way'.[4] These novels challenge directly the feminist critic's expectation of hearing the true voice of women's experience behind the clamour of competing ideologies, of seeing the true face of womanhood beneath the masks of femininity: they challenge the adequacy of sex-role theory, in effect. Stead even provides in each novel a sketch of the contrary view that we all only ever act parts, and that perhaps the quality of that self-fulfilment depends on the quality of the script chosen: Mathilde, Letty's mother, only ever shows her strength when she is reliving her days as an actress, before she became a mother; and Eleanor remembers playing the part of Lady Teazle, when a student, as the most intensely lived moment of her life.

If we read these portraits, instead, to learn how middle-class women have been culturally constructed in English and US society in the first half of the twentieth century, then both *Letty Fox* and *Miss Herbert* emerge as *historical* novels of a kind that are especially interesting to feminists. Each of them is 'a complete social stereotype— the woman of the women's magazines', in the words of one critic, who discusses *Letty Fox* as a novel 'more about the processes of socialization than it is about individual experience, or... the relations between the self and its experience'.[5] And if we attend closely to their claims to representativeness, we can read as well in their narratives trenchant analyses, in a kind of allegorical form, of these whole societies. Their ordinariness and representativeness are established by the accumulation of linguistic detail that precisely identifies the working of contemporary sexual, political and social ideologies. Letty and Eleanor both contribute to the public articulation and circulation of these discourses, through their work in journalism and publishing, and also live out these meanings in their personal lives. Their wasted educations, unhappy relations with men, lack of political commitment, and retreat into respectable marriage and motherhood, all appear to confirm parodically the dire predictions of those who opposed women's emancipation at the turn of the century. Yet as educated middle-class women in a male world that denies them real freedoms, their choices may be interpreted as rational ones.

Making History

The great events of economic depression, political mobilization, war and reconstruction structure the lives represented in these novels without themselves being elaborately drawn in. At one level, Letty and Eleanor can be seen as allegorical figures representing the dominant responses of their class and nationality to these events.

For Letty, the 'wide-awake New Yorker', to become socialist during her buoyant adolescence in the 1930s means to be youthful and progressive, but it has no social urgency for this indulged child of middle-class survivors for whom the Wall Street crash had meant proceeding to live on debts (p. 116):

We did not want things to remain *in statu quo* for our lifetime ... because, actually, things had been changing since we were born, and we were enthusiastically used to it. Although our parents (my mother, I should say) worried about my *sense of security* (a cant phrase of the time), none of us had ever had that; and it was rather the struggle that made us strong. (p. 278)

What Letty means by 'struggle', however, is not class struggle but a 'Darwinian' notion of life that 'relates me, *Letty-Marmelade-always-in-a-jam*, to the plant in my window-box' (p. 279). A few years later and no longer buoyant but fed up with her romantic encounters and ready to settle down, she complains to her idealistic sister:

I don't want to be a real worker. Why do we have to struggle? I don't believe in the struggle of youth. Things ought to be made easy for us when we are at the height of our powers ... (p. 414)

Shrewd Letty has already pointed out that 'radicalism is the opium of the middle class' (p. 386), and she is a sharp observer of her fellow radicals who, once the war effort was stepped up after Pearl Harbor, had all 'fallen into line with an ungraceful bump and there was no more official iconoclasm'. She cheerfully admits that:

I had enough red blood not to like a lot of things I saw passing under the name of patriotism and the war effort, but I hadn't the guts, folly, or lunacy to go out on my own hook. I had to belong to society. (p. 453)

This was the 'moral bottom, which always comes with the profit-taking hour' (p. 454); rather than take a stand against it, Letty resolves to get with the strength:

> My marshal's baton was once more peeping up out of my
> knapsack and sprouting.... If only I could get in touch with
> a great man of action, if only I could work together with
> men of energy and intelligence, modern men who think the
> way I do. I couldn't do anything with the compatible groups
> in which I was happy but lazy...; and I couldn't do much as
> a stenographer, a special article-writer, or a messenger girl;
> and I couldn't do much, truth to tell, bringing more larval
> human beings into the daylight and worrying about diapers
> and cute little sayings and lisping geniuses for years, at
> least, not at my age. I felt the world was too small for me.
> (p. 456)

This is not a choice between conformity and heroic
action so much as a desire to be one of the boys, for whatever they are doing will be preferable to the limited roles
allocated to women. This classically feminine dilemma is
exacerbated by the wartime conditions, of course, but
when the war is over Letty is more than ready to marry
and have her baby: One can't make a great stir, but one
can be on the side of the angels' (p. 499). Letty has a
phrase for everything, no matter how sharply it might
contradict her previous statements, but this is all of a
piece with her vaunted pragmatism, capacity to respond
to change and to survive through adaptation. This is her
specifically American version of common sense, the
hard-headed *laissez-faire* realism which is the legacy of
nineteenth-century liberalism.

Miss Herbert's appeal to commonsense and realism is
of a different hue from Letty's, but it is the sign of her
conformity to a different society, in England, and to a
different moment in bourgeois ideology, that of Tory
conservatism. Just as Letty's narrative demonstrates the
private and social conditions in which U S Left radicalism
gained and then lost its momentum, so the presentation

of Eleanor's Tory populism shows both the power of its reassuring rationality, and its constitutive force in all areas of this woman's life. She is the woman of the century, 'nothing more nor less than a representation of the home life of Britannia from the Twenties until almost the present day'.[6] She wants to be a good woman, asking nothing more than a 'plain, wholesome life', choosing a 'rational' modern marriage, a business arrangement (p. 90), 'no closed world, but society, neighbours, the stream of time' (p. 73). Populist discourse draws on such organic images as this, as well as recalling the classical liberal terminology of natural rights ('Society wants us to be happy, doesn't it? And it's our natural right. So why shouldn't it all chime together?' p. 12).

The allegorical mode is pronounced in *Miss Herbert* where, for instance, her friend Linda Mack is said to belong to a 'well-to-do Whig family' and to be 'a champion of many liberal causes, of free trade, minority rights, social services, nationalization of industry' (p. 11); and where Eleanor herself is connected through her family to other political alternatives, the vaguely socialist anti-imperialism represented by her father and brother and their not quite self-sufficient 'Commonwealth Farm', and an opposing moral revivalism represented by her mother's membership of the New Religious Society. The political associations of the Society are indicated by the fact that Eleanor's profascist husband is employed by it on mysterious missions all over Europe. Eleanor and he are divorced, appropriately enough, during the course of the Second World War, yet she continues in her mild but deadly way to share his views, refusing to countenance ' "bogey" talk of fascism renascent', declaring that the people in 'those camps' were only 'Communists and such fomenters of disorder and gypsies and such who are outsiders anywhere' (p. 166).

During this period of the war, Eleanor is forced to confront doubt and disorder on both personal and national fronts. Her response to the war is identical to her bewilderment about the failure of her marriage:

> 'Did I marry the wrong man? . . . It's as if there's something I don't understand, but I do understand, I face all my problems squarely'. . . 'What if we go down? If it's all been for nothing? If we've all been wrong? Can I live in a world where the British Empire does not live?' (pp. 164-5)

It is said that 'she never recovered from those days, she never recovered her self-possession' (p. 167). In the second half of the novel her life and, by implication, England's, go downhill all the way in aimless muddling and inefficient hard work. After the war, when she tries to earn a living by selling her literary talents on Grub Street, consumed by the passion of 'guinea fever', she ends up working for a petty political spy, feeding him information about the personal lives of her Leftist acquaintances.

She takes on the mindlessly conservative ideological role attributed to middle-class English women by political pundits of the Right and Left, and she takes it on with enthusiasm. She is a dyed-in-the-wool Tory populist, sentimentally patriotic about 'old England' but passive in the face of change.[7] Believing that 'change comes by itself', Eleanor criticizes as 'rash rank outsiders' those who would intervene in this natural process and cause disorder, people like her father, brother and sister-in-law. They, meanwhile, contradict her claim that England is 'a perfectly free society', arguing that 'covert understandings had repressed thoughts and thoughts had dwindled and died' (p. 131). The statement is as true for Eleanor as it is for the country: both suffer intellectual atrophy.

Not to mention sexual atrophy. Eleanor believes there is a clear-cut choice for a woman between passionate love and respectable marriage, but on the way to the latter she allows herself a string of aimless sexual encounters, satisfying her curiosity and testing her capacity to attract men. She justifies her actions as 'striking a blow for freedom' (p. 29) or, later, romanticizes her past as 'struggle and dreams and youth' (p. 89). (It is interesting to see in her notes that one of the alternative titles Stead considered for this novel was 'The Lady and the Slut'.)[8] Much later, as a divorced woman, the separation between her scattered masturbatory fantasies and sentimental friendships with men is bridged by the narcissistic relationship with Quaideson, the old man who watches her pose and never touches her. She is finally able to feel 'perfectly feminine' in the gaze of this necrophiliac admirer, posing among his collection of ancient torture instruments (p. 288). In her, as Helen Yglesias wrote, 'private and social anguish mesh perfectly.'[9]

Eleanor's life touches significant social and political conflicts of her times, yet events in the public sphere scarcely impinge on her consciousness. She remains calm, like a somnambulist, or, when aroused, becomes merely confused. At the same time, the story of her life comes to represent a specific response to those events, specified through the national, class and gender ideologies in which it is told. It is through the silences and the contradictions in this ideological texture that the meaning of political events and personal desires and fears can be understood.

With Letty, in contrast, everything is said, but nothing is reflected upon. The metaphor for *her* text is a visual rather than verbal one. She is, by her own admission, short-sighted and cannot see very far ahead: 'if I could only see clearer ahead, I'd make my way with a straight mind, for I can always look myself in the face and add one and one' (p. 44). Here, then, the first-person narrative allows for both direct social criticism of sexual-economic hypocrisies and, through the revelation of the narrator's short-sightedness, indirect criticism of the ideologies which inform her commonsense realism.

The discourses of common sense constantly produce new forms, such as the cant phrases that Eleanor draws on (and reproduces in her own magazine stories) to regulate social and personal exchanges. Here, for instance, her rules meet some resistance, and her angry reaction finds immediate expression in a racist accusation against her German husband, Henry:

> Over and over again she had read that 'before dinner just one glass of sherry...is correct...' She had written it herself. 'More leads to raised voices and flushed faces'. Now, mortified, in her mind accusing the immoderate habits of Continentals, she went away ('slipped away' she thought to herself) and put on the dinner; Henry should not have the second bottle of sherry. (p. 107)

On many occasions, her rules are resisted by some unrecognized, unacknowledged part of herself, which interrupts the constant process of editing her reactions in conformity to the ideological norms of femininity:

> ...[T]o her confusion, indignant phrases repeated themselves in her mind while she recalled scenes which had left her sore—even though she had always been considerate, sensible, humane and 'exercised her saving sense of humour'.... A scene. In the original: 'Henry, what you call self-reliance and self-control, I call plain self... you retire into this self-sufficiency, to humiliate me. I won't be humiliated.' This mental record ran quickly through, and she edited as it ran, till it then took on its enduring form: 'Henry dear, let us just sit down awhile and thrash this thing out....'Henry then ideally replied, 'I admit I am too

self-sufficient ... You have a better form of it, self-reliance. A mother is closer to the human race.' ... But this rainbow interchange was coarsely interrupted by fierce words hurtling across her mind: 'He gets the best end of the stick and leaves me all the dirty work. He's a brute, the cold little climbing devil.' (p. 111)

Like Letty, too, she has a phrase for everything, and all the phrases can be traced to contemporary discourses on psychology, politics, and so on. They could, theoretically, *all* be enclosed in quotation marks. But it is more than that. Rather, the phrases make her, they *are* her reactions. Stead's writing, in all the later texts but especially in these two, repeatedly demonstrates that we are constructed by language, that language makes us rather than we it, in the sense that it gives a material existence to emotions and ideas which could not otherwise be knowable.

Letty's difference from Eleanor, which could be read as a national as well as a temperamental difference, is that she is aware that these social rules and recipes rarely work, and inevitably contradict one another. She is an expert on women's rules for knowing and controlling men, having listened since babyhood to her deserted mother's friends ('these gossips and pocket Machiavellis') offering useless advice to the luckless Mathilde (p. 61). Letty's training is thorough, and she learns from a variety of sources apart from family gossip. As a schoolgirl, she learns to extract money from her father to help her 'meet the right boy' and get established:

Every magazine in the country was on my side. They all showed a slick, amusing Powers model gouging money out of smooth Papas for clothes, motor-cars, hair-dos, and society colleges. (p. 228)

Stead makes it perfectly clear that realities are constructed, not given, and that their construction is a function of social institutions such as the media and the education system. She also, in Eleanor, makes it clear that, whether we allow ourselves to recognize it or not, we are never passive victims of this socialization process but rather use what we need. But it is social not moral criticism that results for, as another character puts it in *Cotters' England*, a hungry mind will feed on garbage if that is all there is available.[10] One thing that makes Letty's story more enjoyable to read than Eleanor's is that her garbage is more interesting: it includes wisecracks and jokes, and its effect is mostly comic. The effect of recounting Miss Herbert's socialization as a lady tends instead to the absurd.

Everywoman's Guide to Sex and Marriage

Sex and love are central preoccupations in both these portrait novels. Through Letty, Stead analyses the sexual economics of middle-class marriage in all its sordid detail. It is women's business in life to 'know men', and yet Letty knows that the men do what they like (despite groans of anguish from charmers like her father Solander and Uncle Philip), while the women merely survive, their professed high morality inevitably at variance with their actions, and ranged against each other in the competition for men:

> Impossible to become corrupt in this school for girls, for no one had the recipe for getting anything. Even Grandmother's recipe for getting Solander back had not yet worked, and Grandmother didn't seem to care much. (p. 110)

It is Grandmother who offers Mathilde the cynical fruits

of her wisdom, that is, that with two small children to raise and no money of her own, she cannot afford the luxury of love. That must wait until she can pay for it: ' "When you're forty or forty-five, it'll be time to think about necking and—,, her voice softened—"love—and men—and all that" ' (p. 107). This principle of robust submission to the conditions of life for women in a world run by men becomes Letty's guide.

Letty's picaresque tale, from her childhood onwards, is a 'veritable encyclopedia of the relations between men and women',[11] and there are few novels in English before the 1970s which have been so matter of factly frank about taboo subjects like female sexual aggression, male impotence, or the fatal combination of a woman's erotic obsession with a man who is 'a tease, a hound of love' (p. 360). Unlike the sexual autobiographies of the 1970s, however, these experiences are not given the status of major narrative turning-points, measures of the heroine's approach to selfhood, but are represented in the picaresque mode as brief episodes. But, although never elaborated in detail, they are made significant as illustrating Letty's theory of the material basis of love:

'You know love isn't something mystic; it's a bloody real thing, there's nothing realer; and it grows out of all that madness at night, that growing together in the night, that thing without eyes, but with legs, that fit of convulsions, all that we had—' (p. 488)

A different kind of love is set against this theory in Letty's sister Jacky's passion for old men, in particular Gondych, whom she imagines as a modern Faust, herself as Marguerite. It is interesting that Stead's manuscript notes relating to this novel contain a great deal more material on this theme, and it recurs in other notes on a fable of a woman's sexual initiation and obsession.[12] These notes also include more explicit sexual descriptions than any she published, whereas in this novel there is a dramatic separation between Jacky's apparently unfulfilled passion (much like Teresa's in *For Love Alone*) and Letty's varied sexual encounters with men. Yet it is Letty, not her sister, who fears her own capacity for insatiable desire and for whom marriage offers safety, a rest from sexual tourism.

The second part of Letty's story, 'On My Own', is mainly concerned with her experiences of what Grandmother succinctly calls 'the tourist business', that is, free love as invented by men. What promises to be an exploratory journey into unknown and exotic country turns out to be expensive, repetitive and often painful, and after a few years Letty is more than ready to go home. Her recurrent images of herself as a ship indicate the contradictions of her position as a 'free woman'. When her freewheeling life goes well, she sees herself as a pleasure boat cruising from one port to another leaving the dullards behind on the wharf holding broken streamers (p. 424). When a string of disastrous love affairs and an abortion leave her feeling depressed, she thinks that:

> the woman looking for love is like a little boat meeting waterspout after waterspout. She is tired of steering, rowing, looking for land, hanging up old shirts for sails and the rest of it. But the pirates, they are not tired at all.... Perhaps I would weather the troubles and begin to regard men and their passions merely as trade winds. (p. 376)

The world of men is her element, but she is unhappy floating aimlessly around in it. She wants a chance to fulfil her proper purpose:

> I was no hulk nor ghost-ship, but a good freighter made to carry bread and bibles around the world; I was a good, deep

draught, built on dependable old-fashioned lines, no victory ship, no canal boat, and no ship of the line. But a freighter doesn't particularly care for the heaving billow; a freighter has a destination .... (p. 388)

To be good is to be useful, for this child of the New World, and so marriage and pregnancy confer on Letty the self-respect she had felt lacking. It's notable, however, that for all her talk of great men, she is not looking for a pilot, only for a freight; and in the end she believes she has found this in maternity, what she was looking for all along, 'union with something, an ideal, a lover' (p. 499).

She respects, she declares, 'not only my present position, but also all the efforts I made, in every direction, to get here' (p. 502). Her morality is much the same as that attributed to Moll Flanders two hundred years earlier, and it serves a similar purpose, to reveal a situation essentially unchanged since the eighteenth century. Prostitution is the inevitable by-product of a 'free' marriage market where women's economic and social vulnerability obliges them to sell themselves to the highest bidder, the 'free woman' being the one who hires herself rather than selling outright. Like Moll, Letty defends the system with a stoical realism that allows for little self-pity, even less compassion for other women, and no possibility of rebelling against it:

I do not even see a scandal in this, for wide-awake women. In other times, society regarded us as cattle or handsome house slaves; the ability to sell ourselves any way we like is a step towards freedom; we are in just the same position as our Negro compatriots—and they would not go backwards towards their miserable past. (p. 5)

Letty's cheerful acceptance of capitalism's commodication of everything, and her Roosevelt-like rhetoric about taking the good with the bad and looking towards the future, require an immense capacity for self-contradiction. One is tempted to see this, as Elizabeth Perkins does, as the clue to Letty's psychology as a 'converter of facts' who constantly reconstructs reality according to her needs.[13] Or one can read it as a clue to her times, to the fluctuations of political fashion. Yet what it also does—and this is primary in the novel as a literary fiction—is constantly to unsettle the established hierarchy of truths, weighing them all equally whether the language in which they materialize is banal or profound. It becomes impossible to extract from this levelling of discourses the kinds of moral affirmations that literary critics most frequently demand from fiction.

The problem posed by reading this text is similar to that posed by Defoe's Moll Flanders, as others have remarked[14]—How reliable is this first-person narrator? What is the centre of value in all this flux of detail? Letty has been judged 'a self-righteous bitch and a heartless betrayer'.[15] Yet she can equally be regarded as managing to survive and to stay human by playing the rules of the game—and by being lucky. Another reader takes her at her own description as a 'generous fool' who is instrumental in revealing social folly.[16] Readers tend to emphasize either her iconoclasm, her refusal to 'live the way a woman ought to live according to male mythology, or to point out that 'neither does she live the way a woman ought to be able to live'.[17] In this open situation, the reader's judgement of the character determines which narrative mode is identified as dominant; a satirical analysis of the rules of the game by a shrewd player, a revelation of social folly by a 'generous fool', or a comic study in female bad faith.[18]

Passion: Verdi with Mills and Boon

With Eleanor Herbert the problem of how to read the
heroine is exacerbated: the option of seeing her as a
social critic in her own right is not available, and she is
consistently the object of the novel's satire. She arouses
pity, then disgust, then a kind of shocked amusement.
She is surely one of the most disconcerting heroines in
fiction, and this is one of the most curious novels, with
its pastiche of popular discourses and a predominant
comic effect that is mordant rather than scintillating.

Yet some readers conceive her as a tragic figure in
that her attempts to 'measure down' to the middle-class
norm of femininity demonstrate such a waste of
energy,[19] and it has been further suggested that her
refusal of passionate love is a measure of that waste—
that the possibility of love provides the novel with a
centre of value.[20] This feminist reading seeks a fictional
resolution of the contradictions set in play by Stead's
characters in their capacity for love, even if this capacity
goes unrealized. Can we, then, take Letty at her word
that her life's voyage is only now beginning? Can we
read Eleanor's life as a tragedy of unfulfilled passion? It
is true that she is presented as an unawakened Venus,
that her life is a series of shabby failures and hypocrises
which appear to be the consequences of her having
chosen conformity. Yet, as I have already suggested,
there is little narrative encouragement to read her story
as either a tragedy or a moral condemnation of the
unfulfilled life, for the moral condemnation is ultimately
directed at a society which could set such rules, and
Eleanor is too enthusiastically part of it to be tragic.

Nevertheless there is something about the writing in
the two incidents where passion enters her life which
singles them out from the insistent ordinariness of the
prose throughout *Miss Herbert*. With a sudden shift in

register to language signifying passion, all that has been absent from the rest of the narrative seems to emerge, like the return of the repressed, an eruption of utopian desire and the fear of death. Eleanor's response to certain men each time shakes the foundations of her rational common sense, but each time she rejects passion, and in similar terms: it was 'a threat, like a premonition of disease' (p. 44) that would ruin her life, it would be like submitting to 'the hand of fate' (p. 73); it was 'as if a new world came somewhere near her world and she felt its attraction and feared to be pulled away off the earth, out of life' (p. 304). This cosmic, mystical language suggests that Eleanor may be read as a development of the character type Stead has one of her characters in *The Beauties and Furies* describe as a 'complex, subtle nature—chiefly latent, though, so that her will only appears in common rational-mystic forms known to dream doctors and psychiatrists'.[21] That is, the mystical powers which are attributed to passion are the other side of the coin from her determinedly one-dimensional rationalism; the same might be said of the contrast between Letty's 'realism' and Jacky's idealism *vis-à-vis* love and sex.

Side by side with Eleanor's fearful responses to the man, there occurs in each incident a passage of hallucinatory images of pleasure. The first of these encounters occurs in a church, at a wedding:

> She might have been asleep hearing a dream symphony, the people and church swirled round her in a stately circle. Thoughts went through her mind that had never been part of her before: There are side booths, confessionals, I suppose, thousands of lives have been lived before me.... Just streaming out into what's far away. And those to come—a cataract of light! Ages and ages of people....
> These stray ideas were as fragrant and delightful to her

as patches of low-growing flowers on a forest floor.... A great quiet wind blowing round and round her on which the church and audience were dim paintings from past time, carried before her eyes, recollections, images and breaths of passion, like sprays of flowers.... (pp. 44-5)

The imagery recalls Teresa's epithalamium, her vision of time floating away like a river in full flood, a vision which is only reached by breaking through the 'iron circle' of individual consciousness, and by breaking the social/moral law, even risking 'madness'.[22] Kinetic images (swirling, streaming, blowing) suggest bodily sensation as well as violent mental and emotional activity, and this pattern recurs in the second such incident, towards the end of the novel when, as a woman of fifty, Eleanor meets her daughter's lover at the opera:

Her heart had begun a great circular thrumming, so it felt. Round and round it gadded, making larger swoops, ... as if she were floating, with her large body, round the great dome. Her heart began pounding out hard and real thoughts, like pieces of metal, too; and she heard them, forceful, unanswerable: This is love and he knows it; it would be too strong for me, my life would be carried away into a whirlpool, round and round and down, in the centre, lost and gone.... There'd be no meaning to the world or time, but this hour and the future hours with him would break into everything, flooding everything, everything would be washed away...(p. 304)

Like the church setting on the previous occasion, the music provides a structure within which both her vertiginous fear—of losing control, of chaos and death—and her intimations of pleasure can be accommodated. Might this be read as an implicit comment on the role of art?

Yet there is a more troubling question here than that

of the role of passion in the novel's structure or the character's psychology, and it is a question of the codes of representation.[33] Both these moments of passion in the novel are marked by the appearance of a further discourse, distinguishable from the cosmic and kinetic imagery quoted above. It is a sub-Lawrentian or Mills and Boon discourse on sexual attraction:

> But he had looked at her and she at him with the same intensity and knowledge that an animal has, when it looks straight into the eyes of a human, a meaningless but profound and moving look. (pp. 42–3)

and again, her daughter's fiancé, meeting her:

> looked straight into Eleanor's eyes with the glance of a man who understands a woman wants him and who gives himself and means to take all, a dark look that existed long before language. (p. 303)

At this point we have not only to deal with this recognizable code of commodified sexual mysticism, but also with the shift to a projected masculine point of view, to the male gaze ('a man who understands...'). It is difficult for readers to know where we stand.

What is more, the opera is Verdi's *La Forza del Destino*. The narrative's only comment on this fact is the aside, 'for some reason Eleanor always called it *La Sforza del Destino*' (p. 302). The slip is revealing, for *sforza*, effort or exertion, is the keynote of her own destiny: it is what she substitutes for this fearful submission to fate. Her namesake in the opera, Leonora, on the other hand, follows the dictates of passion and brings about the deaths of her father and brother as well as herself. If this is Western culture's story of the woman who commits herself to passion, perhaps Eleanor is right to leave it well alone. The parodic effect established by this mixture of popular sexual-mystical language and allusion to high culture's representations of tragic passion puts in question the possible status of passion as authentic, or a moral centre.

Yet these 'parallel texts' of popular and high culture are both products of a patriarchal culture, representations of a femininity which in fact serves to elicit male desire and subsequent action. They both signify male desire, and so raise the problem of how *female* desire may be signified by such cultural codes, a question addressed in the novel itself. The allusion to Verdi's Leonora recalls another story mentioned in *Miss Herbert*, the novel written by her father about Sabrina, the consumptive *femme fatale* who makes all the men in the village fall in love with her, and ruins them (p. 168). Obviously, it flatters Eleanor's fantasy of her power to attract men, particularly as she has renounced this eroticized image of woman since her marriage and taken on its complement in patriarchal iconography, the image of the asexual and censoring mother. There are, of course, no reflections of this kind in the text—only the throw-away line: 'the story was tender, forgiving, like a man writing about his daughter'. The *femme fatale* (like Leonora) represents disorder and ultimately death for men, and if Eleanor is flattered by the story's representation of Woman, she is perhaps even more attracted by its tender tone because, as we have seen earlier, a daughter may need forgiveness from the father for being a woman at all. Eleanor's father's choice of the name Sabrina for his heroine recalls the chaste nymph in Milton's 'Comus', defender of women's 'honour' and controller of the stream of life. Such a woman might be especially pleasing to a jealous father.

Eleanor's response is to take the book over: she revises

it, writing in the 'female psychology', but there is some
quarrel about the latter, her father maintaining that
'every man has something feminine in him', and then she
has to rewrite again to suit editors' demands for 'reader
identification' and 'common coin'. Finally it is published,
as *Brief Candle*, 'not much noticed but well sold'
(pp. 169–70).

This aspect of the incident links it to other instances of
literary satire, parody and pastiche in *Miss Herbert*. There
is the saccharine story which Eleanor produces at her
father's suggestion that she write about her own anger,
'the story of the ill-treated wife'. Its very title, 'Deb and
Russ [her children] at Sunnytop Farm' recalls the classic
tear-jerker, *Rebecca of Sunnybrook Farm*, just as the title of
Brief Candle suggests popular writers of the period like
Howard Spring. (And, incidentally, the title of *Letty Fox:
Her Luck* recalls countless Victorian schoolgirl novels.)
Eleanor's mother's favourite author, Elinor Glyn,
provided her as a child with information about sexuality,
just as the short stories in women's magazines later
provide her with guides to action as well as formulas for
her own writing ('How true, thought Eleanor, there is
humble truth under these banalities. It had meaning for
romantic women like herself.... She extracted the
outline and rewrote the story a little,' p. 39). The final
third of the novel, her Grub Street period, abounds with
gems such as this, from one of her reader's reports:
'...he has a kind of intuition of genius and we must put
our foot down firmly there, or it will ruin his talent'
(p. 291). The object of the novel's satire expands from
Eleanor herself to encompass the literary world and the
commodities it produces for sale, its promiscuous
mixtures of 'Verdi and Mills and Boon' and their material
effects on the woman who attempts to live by it and its
values.[24]

These two novels, *Miss Herbert* and *Letty Fox*, may be

read as cautionary tales for women, as answers to the liberal feminists of an earlier period who believed that emancipation into an idealized notion of the public world would at last allow women to fulfil themselves. Among twentieth-century women novelists Christina Stead is the great ironist of female experience. Her fictions not only criticize patriarchal capitalist social structures and their ideologies but also insist that women are neither immune from their corruptions nor their passive victims. Her women characters are shown to be capable of exploiting others—and of simultaneously denying that they do so. They are shown to be accomplices in the suppression of their own desires and the construction of oppressive ideologies of femininity. The utopian possibility of love as a mode of knowledge for women rather than a romantic or a picaresque tale, which emerges in *For Love Alone*, does not reappear in her post-war novels. In these satirical portraits, knowledge and love appear in the form of ready-made ideological constructions of reality. The theme of struggle takes the form of a struggle for 'normal' social existence, rather than creative engagement. In the final two novels to be considered here, we see something more like a life-and-death struggle for survival—there is blood on the floor, and 'love', along with 'politics', can be a murder weapon.

Chapter Five

Monstrous Passions:
I'm Dying Laughing and
Cotters' England

Christina Stead's post-war novels show a deep disillusionment about the possibilities for social liberation
that had invigorated European and United States
cultural and political life during the years between the
two world wars. Disillusionment is not quite the word
for such a clear cold eye as hers, but let it serve to point to
a shared political crisis which turned some on the Left
into apologists for the status quo, like the Howards in *I'm
Dying Laughing*, and sent others into mysticism, like Nellie
at the end of *Cotters' England*.[1] Instead, Stead might be said
to have settled down 'for the duration' of the Cold War
to write a critical-fictional history of that period of
retreat, through the everyday lives of people who
experienced it. Within her habitual focus on the
everyday seen in close-up, they enact power struggles at
the personal/sexual level at the same time as they
rehearse, endlessly, public/political debates around
events 'off-stage'.

The Personal and the Political

Bringing together these two novels produces another comparison and contrast between England and the U S and, just as with *Letty Fox* and *Miss Herbert*, a dominant political discourse and practice can be discerned in each. In *Cotters' England*, the struggles and defeats of social democracy in an England devastated by war exhaustion, problems of housing, malnutrition, and war injuries both physical and emotional; and in *I'm Dying Laughing*, the falling star of post-war U S communism which, for the Howards after their escape to Paris, sheds its fading light on the complex moral dilemmas facing the European survivors of imprisonment, occupation and resistance.

These recent histories form the texture of the lives told in fiction. They are interwoven with the melodramatic commonplaces beloved of their protagonists ('Life/love is an incurable disease', Nellie Cotter; 'I'm dying laughing', Emily Howard) and, as well, with residues from older stories—of the American dream and the French Revolution (Emily, a 'Danton in skirts',[2] is haunted by the sound of the tumbrils); and folk-tales of ghosts and other spirits of place in ancient England.[3] As always, the social and the historical are never merely background fillers but are part of the characters' discursive construction of their dilemmas, clichés included.

Each is a woman-centred history, and the female protagonist in each case is a great monologist, though not a first-person narrator. Stead expands the scope of these 'historical novels' by expanding the narrative beyond the voice of the female protagonist. Nellie Cotter is surrounded by family, neighbours and followers, and her brother Tom takes up almost as much of the action as she—though she has the monopoly on talk. Emily Howard's relationship with her husband is as central as Nellie's with Tom and she, too, is surrounded by family, colleagues and (given the Howards' style of life), 'paid help'. As the cast in each case is larger so, too, is the number of perspectives available on the action.

Neither narrative is as consistently satirical as the two portraits, and therefore each lacks a defined object of criticism (whether a stereotype, a political position, or the social structure that produces these). Rather than satire, there is an intensification of the process, noticed in the portrait narratives, of shifting ironic perspectives without ever producing a stable or unified position of knowledge for the reader. The subtler and polyphonic ironies in *Cotters' England* and *I'm Dying Laughing* constitute a narrative mode which extends the critical challenges discussed in the previous chapter. The reader is more often aware of the instability of her position, and without certainty about where the emphasis falls. Specifically, we are required to ask what connections can be made between the sexual politics represented in close-up and the public/political events and debates to which the characters constantly allude. And for feminist criticism in particular, with its vital links to the slogan, 'the personal is political', the crucial question is: how can the psychical and the social be seen to connect at the level of discourse? Most critics of *Cotters' England* have simply separated off the personal from the political aspects of the novel and described them separately.[4] Similarly, Australian reviews of the recently published *I'm Dying Laughing* have tended to greet it as a major political novel, leaving Emily's tormented relationship to her husband and his inheritance either for separate comment, or out of account altogether.[5]

On the other hand, satisfactorily establishing connections is no simple matter. For instance, to suggest that the personal relationship causes the political betrayal, or vice versa, would be to assume a causal relation between the two factors that is bound to place them in a hierarchy of determining power. Alternatively, to collapse the two factors into a single one, to identify them, is equally unsatisfactory because one loses the means of making analytical distinctions between the public/political and the personal/political.

Stead's capacity to knit together, to 'complicate', public and personal themes by means of a formal structure of dramatic ironies has been pointed out in relation to *Cotters' England* by Terry Sturm, but even his elaboration of this idea concludes that it is the formative influence of the Bridgehead past that explains the 'close connection between Nellie's capacity for *self*-deception and her misunderstanding of the social and political character of English working class life'.[6] That is to say, a single determining cause, history, is used to explain that 'complication of... public and personal';[7] and, related to this view of causality, Nellie's political notions are characterized as 'misunderstanding', which implies that if she were not so deceived (in both senses) then she could see truthfully, beyond ideology. Yet, as Sturm himself concludes, Nellie is in the end irreducibly established as a personality despite being 'placed' by the novel's dramatic revelations. The same thing could be said of Emily in *I'm Dying Laughing*. But can this phenomenon only be accounted for by a gesture towards the writer's 'creativity'? Instead, I think, we can learn from her work a more complex model of the operations of ideology in history and in the constitution of subjectivity than it has been possible to learn, until recently, from theoretical texts in Marxism and psychoanalysis.

The exploration of such issues that is possible in fiction is something that recent feminist and socialist criticism attends to, but there is still far to go. Stead's novels constitute a substantial challenge to extend what has been called 'ideological analysis', because they offer us neither classical-realist characters (heroines and victims) nor a distinctively modernist fragmentation of subjectivity and interior drama. Her personages, both male and female, are embedded in, and constructed through, ideologies: the satires *Letty Fox* and *Miss Herbert* (also *A Little Tea, A Little Chat*) demonstrate this most sharply and systematically. Yet they are also marked by a compulsive energy, apparently in excess of ideological contradictions and confusions, by melodramatic speech and behaviour, by obsessively repeated images of desire—hunger, thirst, restless movement. They are more like forces or embodied passions than persons or symbols—forces which, however, are only knowable by means of the specific discourses (historical and ideological) which construct them in culture.

Emily and Nellie: the similarity of their names (and *their* affinity with Ellen, Eleanor, Letty, Elvira) is surely no accident, and nor is the similarity between their symbiotic relationships with weaker males. As well, both women wield power through the word, written and spoken: they are not only journalists by trade but both also have the capacity to seduce as well as to harangue with speech. They both embody, or enact, monstrous passions which are identifiably feminine ones. It is as if, by smashing the mirrors of all the available 'good woman' images, they take on their ideological opposites—harpy, witch, monster, female Caliban.[8] More than this, though—it is no mere question of labels or stereotypes—they proceed to enact these roles with huge gusto, to the imminent destruction of others as well as themselves. If they are vengeful furies, what crimes are they avenging? If their exercise of power constitutes misrule, chaos and disorder, what is its dynamic and its social significance? Does it merely invert patriarchal oppositions, or does it point to the possibility of displacing the system of gender oppositions itself? Feminist criticism has two major clusters of concerns. The first may be defined as an enquiry into cultural constructions of femininity and the relations of women as social subjects to language and other signifying systems. The second, like feminist critiques of other established forms of knowledge, questions the limits set to literary criticism's own project by its patriarchal nature, and its capacity to deconstruct its implicit hierarchy of rationality, coherence, identity, and so on. The issues raised by these two novels lead us in both directions, and both sets of concerns inform the discussion which follows.

'Cotters' England'

The all-too-rare combination of a political novel with a female protagonist is even more remarkable in this case because the characters are almost exclusively working-class. To describe Nellie Cotter as a left-wing journalist of working-class origins who is also centrally concerned with the oppression of women might suggest that Stead has set up a protagonist capable of dealing with the structurally enmeshed conflicts of class and gender in a 'progressively' feminist and socialist way. Yet although this description of Nellie is literally true, she functions in the novel to exacerbate and compound these conflicts. For she is also accurately described as an unscrupulous, domineering sentimentalist whose socialism consists of bemoaning the people's 'wasted lives' while denigrating the work of her activist colleagues, and whose feminism involves kowtowing to men's faces while she ridicules them behind their backs, and manipulating her influence over other women while she professes all sympathy for 'the pathetic imprisoned Eves'. Again, though, she is more than this caricature, for she is fascinatingly awful and fatally charming. Other characters describe her as a 'sobsister', a 'phoney', 'corrupt'—and also 'a loving soul', a true friend, an heroic battler. She is funny and compelling, a wit as well as a witch. Often self-parodying, she is saved from caricature by the force of her passion, her ferocious egotism, like all Stead's unforgettable egomaniacs. Her survival at the end of the novel, after a succession of deaths, reminds one of Sam Pollit. The novel is very definitely *her* 'psychological drama of the person'.

The opening scenes economically introduce major issues and images, characteristic interchanges and juxtapositions. Nellie, having a dress fitting in the front room of her London house, stands around in 'her cotton shirt and long fleecy bloomers', smoking and talking constantly, interrupting herself with paroxysms of coughing. She is making herself known to Camilla Yates, the dressmaker, who lives opposite:

> 'I was told the other day I'd lost all me personality since I married George. But marriage is an incurable disease; and it drives out the others.'
> Mrs Yates said it was not incurable. (p.9)

Camilla's calmly sceptical responses to Nellie's pronouncements show up their extravagance but make no impression on her: 'incurable disease' is one of her favourite phrases, applied equally by Nellie and her protégées to life (p.39), to love (p.87), to missing her husband (p.224), to someone else's suicidal despair (p.275)—and to the venereal disease she convinces one friend she has caught (p.79). 'Incurable disease' is Nellie's key phrase, signifying the unalterable and terminal condition of hunger, suffering and fear which she constantly conjures with her words. While others engage in political struggle to right wrongs, 'Nellie had chosen Bedlam and the lazaret as brothers and sisters' (p.294).

Camilla's silent presence in this scene by no means impedes the flow of Nellie's talk, and within a few pages we have been introduced to her family and her current obsession with Caroline, the young middle-class woman with whom she has been working on a new housing estate ('a beautiful soul, Camilla', 'she's known the tragedy of failure and the dead end of the lonely road', p.14). There is her husband, George Cook, who is away 'living on the fat of the land, touring the world as a representative of the working class of Great Britain' (p.10)—but whom Nellie praises in the next breath: 'Eh, what a bloody egotist, love; but what a man!...the perfect marriage, the perfect counterpoint' (p.12).

Her pet phrases recur, and the contradictions abound as Nellie moves on to the generation gap ('Our parents', she said, 'were poor, pitiful, frail human creatures', p.17), and her brother Tom, who is both a 'puir la'ad' and 'a spendthrift, a ne'er-do-well, an unemployable, a mischief-maker', whose love for Marion is described as his 'iron ration of happiness' but also in terms of imprisonment by the spider woman: 'She's taken the poor helpless fly and made him her parcel' (p.18).

Camilla is, despite her resistances, 'won by the inner melody of the northern voice and its unexpected cry, its eloquence' (p.17). This seduction by the voice recurs throughout, to all the characters, and Tom shares his sister's magic: 'this pair, the singing brother and the singing sister'. Caroline sees Nellie sympathetically, once, as 'singing for herself, a nightingale, the victim of her song...it did not seem to matter who heard' (p.262). But we are shown from the beginning that the listener does matter, and there is always an element of calculation in it, as here: '[Nellie] cocked her head, like a journalist envisaging his paragraph' (p.17). It is already clear that the contradictions in what she says are due to her desire sometimes to dazzle and bamboozle others, sometimes to tell them what they want to hear, sometimes to tell herself what she wants to believe. Nellie's voice is like an echo-chamber.

As it slowly dawns on Camilla (and the first-time reader) that Marion is dying of cancer and that her wandering life with Tom is in search of a cure, Nellie has already deflected her jealous hostility into an account of her own supreme importance to Tom's life—an account of their youth in Bridgehead which sets the groundwork for all the rest, though not always in ways which Nellie recognizes:

> 'I'm the guilty one. I brought him to London from the home climate and everyone doesn't transplant. I was the pathfinder. I thought I'd go out and find a way for them, my brother and sister.... So I influenced them too much perhaps. I knew I had something in me. Aye, I was guilty. I walked out of a good job with me poor mother depending on me pay. Me dad, the old soldier, was wearing out his strength lifting the elbow. He made good money but it went down the gutters of Bridgehead one way and another. Ah, the grand old humbug; he's been the plague of our lives. I never liked it here, pet. They still make me feel like an invader from the north. But I had to come. It was my destiny. There it is, pet, in a nutshell. Now you understand us.'
>
> 'Is it cancer?' said Camilla. (pp.19-20)

Nellie's myth of origin is a myth of power: her sense of guilt at leading Tom and Peggy astray in their youth (it is never specified how, only linked to the mysterious figure of Jago) doubles as a belief in her right to control their lives in the present. The myth of her leadership contains elements of sacrifice, too (leaving behind her parents, and a sentimentalized idea of 'the north'), although her references to Ma and Pop Cotter are always ambivalent.

The novel's second scene is set in Bridgehead, on Nellie's visit to her ailing mother, and it soon sets up further complexities and hints at further secrets. For instance, the position of the Cotters as respectable working class is quickly sketched by reference to the front room furniture, which includes a piano and an 'expensive leather suite' (p.22). This sketch is later filled in by references to the furniture repayments and genteel poverty having taken priority over decent food, and references to the parents' fear of offending their neighbours or creating any kind of sexual scandal. At the same time, secrets within the family are suggested by Nellie's fawning relationship to her father, her bullying of Peggy and her strange sexual aggression towards old Uncle Simon, where she strips down to wash at the kitchen sink in front of him, insisting that 'We're all guilty, you and me too. We're all guilty' (p.29). Bridgehead family dynamics underlie the exploitative sexual politics favoured by Nellie and Tom in their different ways.

The Bridgehead class structure informs the different inflections of 'socialist politics' signified by Nellie's romantic defeatism and George's bluff opportunism, by Tom's desertion of the cause and by the ineffectual doorknock campaigns against the Bomb to which Eliza (George's first wife) is doggedly committed. The name of the town itself—a bridgehead being an advanced position established in or near enemy territory—might suggest a Leninist notion of the vanguard party necessary to lead the socialist revolution. Ironically, those who revolt against Bridgehead and its respectable pieties and poverty, its 'humbug and humble pie', as Eliza says, must establish their bridgehead in London. But their own disagreements splinter the vanguard: they are rootless, alienated from working-class institutions unless they follow George into reformist unionism or

Eliza into the Communist Party's peace campaign. While George wants to turn his back on England for good, Nellie is absurdly parochial: refusing to write the kind of theoretically-informed journalism her Marxist editor wants, she declares that she will have none of this 'foreign theory' for ' "You can't teach socialism, Camilla; it comes . . . by mysterious ways. . . ." Eliza and Camilla burst out laughing' (p.237).

The second aspect of Bridgehead vanguardism is its underside, the 'Bohemianism' associated with Nellie in the novel, which is presented as anarchistic rebellion against sexual and social respectability. Through Nellie, Bohemianism acquires connotations of both hypocrisy (she is concerned to appear 'perfectly' married, and rages against other women having sexual adventures) and 'the perversity, the nonchalant feeble depravity' which her victim, Caroline, sees in her relationships with lesbian women like Johnny Sterker (p.293).

The mysterious figure of Jago—his name evokes the slums of London's criminal underworld[9]—is seen by the Bridgehead group as the source, in their shared past, of this 'corruption'. He is associated with the imagery of hunger, even starvation, that dominates the text. Eliza assures Nellie that she understands the appeal of such a small-town guru to the young:

> 'I've always had the thought', said Eliza, 'that hunger is a greater passion than love; and I've been surprised not to hear them talk about the distortions produced by hunger, the sublimations and disguised forms of hunger. . . . So it must take very diverse forms in us, especially in a childhood and youth of semi-starvation.' (p.211)

Despite Nellie's sententious dismissal, 'Oh, no, pet . . . Man does not live by bread alone', it is quite clear that Eliza means material hunger, and indeed the associated images are powerfully literal: Tom insists, 'I could live on bread', Nellie subsists on tea, cigarettes and raw onions, Peggy's vegetarianism is one form of revenge she takes on the old people she has been left to care for. The famous set-piece of the aborted chicken dinner draws on all of this, and George Cook's enthusiasm for good food and Continental cuisine is a wickedly appropriate index of his eagerness to leave 'Cotters' England' behind him.

In Cotters' England nobody nurtures, not even the women, and in personal relationships as in politics, it's a matter of 'every man for himself', despite Nellie's crooning and caring. Curiously, though, it is Tom Cotter's ability to present himself as a needy child which arouses a powerful combination of maternal and sexual desire in women: the image of women resting his head between their breasts recurs, yet he never offers to meet their sexual desires as well. He says that Nellie has taken his heart. Cannibalism is more like the order of the day, and the text abounds with references to both Tom and Nellie as vampires.

They are the 'fatal brother and sister' (p.342), as both Caroline and Eliza eventually come to see them, bonded together yet competing for a fantasised power over women—for access to the breast, perhaps. Acting out their own symbiotic relationship, they are like a pair of puppets, constantly repeating themselves. Tom systematically seduces each of Nellie's friends. Nellie repeatedly tells him that his life is unreal, that he is 'dancing in the hall of mirrors', that he is shadow to her truth. Another set-piece in the novel occurs when they go into the Hall of Mirrors at a country fair, and Nellie draws him into a dance where she becomes both mirror and castrating sword: 'her face bright as metal, triumphant, gleamed and cut into him; very bright, her small eyes peered into his large bursting ones' (p.190).

The brother–sister pair is echoed in several ways: in

the bond between Mrs Cotter and her brother Simon, in the *ménage à trois* at Lamb Street where Eliza passes for George's sister instead of his first wife, and the comparable household around Marion and her husband, where both Tom and Patrick claim to be her half-brothers instead of her lovers present and past. As well, an incestuous link across the generations is strongly suggested in relation to both Uncle Sime ('We're all guilty') and Pop Cotter (Nellie 'had to wait till [he] was half dead before the great light shining on her face and blinding her to other men waned', p.270).

A final set of images which works to expand the configuration of Cotters' England beyond the public/political are those that evoke the notion of witchcraft and magic. There is an evocation of pagan England through Tom's lyrics about travelling in the country-side, through the more surreal of his stories, and through his self-description, 'poor Tom's a 'cold' (p.243, p.251), which recalls *King Lear*, both the ancient kingdom and the role of the knowing fool in the play. Tom is associated with the clown and the 'mountebank' (p.260), but none the less with history and human culture, attributes of the masculine side of patriarchal binary opposites. Nellie, in contrast, is associated with *liminal* states—between female and male (when she dresses in Tom's clothing), animal and human (she is imaged in a series of birds, from barnyard hen to stalking marsh-bird), human and supernatural (as harpy, witch, hobbledehoy, devil, with 'me great black and rosy wings' p.345). She is a creature of metamorphosis here:

> Nellie laughed, was so pleased she seemed to fly, eyes winking, hair sticking out like straws, arms akimbo, legs flying about, shoulders waggling, she sketched a fairy hobbledehoy, a woman cut free from the earth. (p.287)

And in the climactic party scene where she rests her harpy's 'beak' on Caroline's shoulder, showing her the metamorphosis of the naked women in the garden below:

> The moonlight showed that some were rosy in the daytime, others were the colors of night-lighted fish and they were like queer fish, a seahorse, an old man snapper, a gar, a toadfish, a puffball and one rather awkward and hesitant was as yet, only a woman.... (p.291)

In this passage, what begins as a joke about 'queer fish', in tune with the moralistic queasiness throughout the text about lesbians and Bohemia, starts to sound like horrified fascination with 'depths' in which moral distinctions are subsumed in the unconscious. The attribution in this text of 'disorder' and 'anarchy' to women living without the love of men (which recurs in other novels as well as in Stead's interviews, as we saw in chapter l) evokes, through the imagery of witchcraft, *all* sexual and egotistic energies as demonic and disruptive. In a novel where the dramatic action is structured around a series of deaths (Marion, both Cotter parents, Caroline, George), there is no possibility held out that order might be restored, or reached. The springs of action lie in Nellie's obsession, and action merely ceases when she leaves the scene, first to join George in Geneva and then, after his sudden death, when she turns her attention to 'the problems of the unknowable' (p.352). The implicit link or parallel between social/political order and psychic/personal order is stretched to its limits.

This expansion of the text's range of signification renders the novel irreducible, I think, to descriptions such as Yglesias's 'why the English working-class movement has not made the revolution'.[10] This is not to deny the relevance of such a comment, however. Similarly, I find it difficult to accept as sufficient Brydon's feminist reading of the novel as an ideological critique of the false consciousness represented by Nellie, through a revelation of the falsity of her ideas, her self-deceptions and deceptions of others:

> Although Stead's characters remain trapped in their hall of mirrors, her readers may feel themselves freed, because ... they can see the hall of mirrors described for what it is—a conjuror's trick. And when the trick is exposed, the illusion vanishes.[11]

The very fact that the image of the distorting mirror is Nellie's favourite one for invalidating other people's realities is perhaps warning against employing such a notion of ideology in analysis. Besides, Nellie's accusations to this effect never succeed in deflecting Tom; and her power to bend others, most horribly Caroline, to her will comes not from providing them with alternative images, but from exploiting the contradictions between various class and gender ideologies so as to disorient them totally.

The concept of false consciousness, and the implied possibility of 'correcting' it in order to see clearly and act freely, employs a pre-psychoanalytic notion of the unconscious as continuous with consciousness and accessible to it. Since Althusser, however, ideology can be understood as the work of making sense of social experience that operates at the level of the Imaginary, something not confined to 'consciousness' (false or otherwise).[12] Thus the unsatisfactory concept of 'false consciousness', with its implication that a stable truth can be discovered beyond its deceptive veils, can be discarded. In arguing for a broader concept of ideology, encompassing its constitutive role in signification and subjectivity, Gayatri Spivak stresses the need to see individual subjects as 'irretrievably plural', though still having the power to act and to resist.[13] Returning to *Cotters' England*, then, we can read the narrative operations of irony differently. The deceptions they reveal will, rather than offering us access to the realm of Truth, construct a multiplicity of competing truths, suggesting the material embodiment of each in particular subjects as well as pointing to the compulsive springs of action in the unconscious.

Part of feminist criticism's inheritance from the humanist tradition is an explanatory model of reading: a hermeneutic tendency to seek out a text's presumed hidden meanings, meanings that will, ideally, cohere around a single unifying or even causal principle such as 'the search for identity' or 'the critique of the patriarchal family'. There are, inevitably, traces of this model in my own and others' readings of Stead's texts. Yet with these two late novels, especially, we are confronted with texts which appear to offer not even provisional schema of explanation: not only do they abound with odd details which 'don't fit', but they appear to have no coherent structure, either. There is only the increasing speed of the protagonist's mania—Stead herself said that she wanted *I'm Dying Laughing* to go 'from fire to more fiery to fierier still'.[14]

Juxtaposition rather than connection, rapid movement (whether in speech or action) rather than reflection and explanation, repetition and accumulation are the dominant techniques, reminiscent of cinema, which increasingly accompany the careful effacement of narratorial presence in Stead's writing. It is important to continue paying attention to these formal means by which the texts construct their meanings. It is all the more important to do so with these political novels, for the modes of explanation that spring most readily to hand are precisely those which will tend to trivialize the

issues—by 'psychologizing' characters, for instance—
thereby 'proving' once again the liberal-humanist
doctrine that politics can never be the stuff of 'literature'.
I'm Dying Laughing poses this problem all the more sharply
because the political context inscribed in it is so widely
known and discussed.

'I'm Dying Laughing: The Humourist'

This novel was not published until after Stead's death,
although she had been working on it intermittently
since the late 1940s. It appears that she put it aside after
settling in London, to work on *Cotters' England* and
Miss Herbert, among other things, but the principal
reason for this delay was that when she submitted it to a
U S publisher in 1966, it was recommended that she fill
out the political context for a generation of readers to
whom the 'McCarthy era' was just a name. She could
never complete the revision to her satisfaction.

Clearly, documentation was not congenial to her, and
we have seen how in the other novels debates and events
are alluded to rather than described and analysed. From
the evidence of her revisions (discussed briefly by editor
Geering in his preface to the novel), it seems that what
she became caught up in was, precisely, a vain effort to
explain the crisis of her characters by tracing their
political and personal commitments back to a point of
origin. The opening chapters are set in 1935 and describe
Emily's and Stephen's meeting at the international
writers' congress in Paris (which Stead herself had
attended with the British delegation).[15] Next there is a
jump to 1945 in Hollywood, where the local branch of
the Communist Party takes them to task over their
deviations (moral as well as political) from party policy;
their subsequent flight to New York is motivated by
intra-party conflict, not McCarthyist persecution. By

the time *that* scenario gets under way they have moved
on to Paris, where the events of the second part of the
novel take place. So it is not so much a novel about
McCarthyism and the American Left as it is about two
American communists, alienated already from their
party, confronted with post-war reconstruction and the
Cold War in Europe. There could be no single
satisfactory starting-point for such a narrative, which is
perhaps why Emily needs to be given a vivid, impression-
istic sense of historical connections which stretches back
to the nineteenth-century origins of the 'American
dilemma' between the desires for social justice and for
wealth and fame, and beyond that to the French
Revolution with its political triumphs and compromises.
Similarly, there could be no sufficiently complex
connections made between their political and their
personal crises to explain the one in terms of the other.
As with *Cotters' England*, there is no single point of origin
for its action and no one frame of explanation for its
outcome.

In contrast to the organizing images of hunger and
poverty in the Cotters' story, in *I'm Dying Laughing* the
Howards' political and personal relationships are dominated by money—getting it and spending it. Plotting
how to get more of it is crucial to the plot of the novel,
and spending it on good food, copious drinks and lavish
parties provides the setting of a majority of its scenes.
It's the world of Letty Fox on a much larger scale. At
times it recalls the fetishized relations to wealth that
Stead explored in *House of All Nations*, where to
manipulate money is to exert power over people, and to
spend it is to achieve a kind of orgasmic release from
sexual anxieties. Here, for instance, the dizzying slide
from persons to things that Emily makes when
reassuring Stephen of her need of him and the children:

'Oh, oh, I need everything so badly, so much, Stephen. I can't do without anything. I need you all. Stephen, let's get a new wallpaper, a good one, and French curtains.' (p.112)

Money is what they fight about, and what they make up with. Emily is the breadwinner because she is a successful popular writer, while Stephen produces important but unremunerative essays on economics and politics. She is proud of this role, but also resents selling her talents for dollars, believing that she could write good serious fiction and blaming the Party as well as Stephen for requiring her earning capacity over her integrity as proof of commitment to the cause. Stephen has renounced his wealthy family and his inheritance by embracing the revolutionary cause, but must continue to live in the grand manner to which he is accustomed, and which Emily enjoys with gusto. Besides, he is guardian to Olivia, his daughter by a former marriage, and a nephew, Christy, both of whom stand to inherit vast sums, so there is a further reason—one which they regard as altruistic—for him and Emily to maintain their luxurious style of living. In this respect they are reminiscent of characters in a Balzac novel.

Money defines the Howards' class position, and that in turn defines their relation to the revolutionary movement. In Hollywood their branch of the Party consists solely of wealthy and powerful writers, segregated not only from other members of the movie industry but also from 'the vulgar Mexican worker downtown', otherwise 'we'd overwhelm, discourage and then drive out the ordinary worker'—to which Emily retorts, 'In flat words, we're rich and he's poor. What good can come of it?' (pp.90-1). When they fall out with this group, Stephen fears losing his sense of purpose—and his place among 'the boys' (p.117)—but Emily feels it immediately in terms of money: she loses contracts at the studios (p.127). Ironically, her successful economic relation to capitalism as a professional radical is threatened by her taking an 'ultra-Leftist' position critical of the Party's populist wartime policies of downplaying class conflict, forbidding strikes, and claiming that 'Communism is twentieth-century Americanism', in the words of Party leader Earl Browder.[16] Later, in Paris, they are unknown to the local Party leaders, and attempt to buy their way into notice by giving extravagant parties. Radicalism may be, as Letty maintained, the opium of the middle class, but it is as expensive as any other drug. Finally, when they can no longer afford it, Emily finds that she has scribbled unconsciously in the margin of her letter of recantation the sum '$30,000', the price for selling out to the Howards (p.403).

Stead's treatment of the couple's changing political stance and its 'complication' in their family and personal relationships is shockingly successful. It successively risks sounding like an anti-communist sob story, a heroic socialist tragedy of persecution, and a satirical attack on her characters and all their kind. Finally, this tale of 'the humourist' is none of these things, but its narrative irony derives largely from the play of their possibilities. It takes off from the brilliant political satire of the Hollywood party scene where Emily and Stephen are 'straightened out' by their colleagues for their ultra-Left deviations. This is the setting, unobtrusively indicating the sexual as well as the party politics in operation:

The women sat about among the men, saying very little, huddling in groups and talking quietly about their children, well-dressed, modern, polite and most somewhat drunk; and the men, also drunk, took many postures, horsing on the backs and arms of chairs, striding up and down, leaning on the windowsills, on the high mantel of the bogus fireplace. As they passed, the women drew in their feet.... Clara Byrd and Emily were boldly drunk. (p.92)

After the accusations the Howards are given the chance to 'reconsider all that you have written and said in a, perhaps, intemperate, ill-considered personal way' because 'we understand why you have taken this diversionist road' (p.95). This 'reason' turns out to be what the sanctimonious Godfrey calls 'the rape of Olivia', by which they mean the Howards' fight for guardianship of the girl and of Christy in order to get their hands on the children's inheritance. But the ultimate target is Emily herself as an 'unfit mother', and their attack takes the form of a paper prepared for the court, a wonderful parody of psychiatric discourse:

'[W]e observed the signs in Emily Howard of a degenerating psychism, of intellectual lesions, perhaps.... There were verbal incontinence, detailed recitals of insignificant events, a general excitement, incoherencies of speech, unsuitable confidences in public—' (p.101)

It is self-evident to Godfrey that Emily's problem is being a woman, though he is surprised and saddened to note that not even 'worldly success and the satisfaction of a woman's deepest instincts' (he means motherhood) have cured her. As he continues, the language modulates into pop psychology and then into a kind of seventeenth-century disquisition on her 'humours':

'Surely before, she had had a lively good humour, a natural comic spirit, a broad general wit, an almost gargantuan perception, an unrepressed genial flow of animal spirits distilled upwards into true wit—'
'Golly, thank you, Godfrey,' said Emily, her fat, mottled red face laughing, though it was set in seriousness.
'—observation, reflection, something unique, the word is not too much. And what is there now? She stammered,

stuttered, emitted long parade speeches turned on instantly as if prepared long before....' (p.102)

The point of quoting this at some length is not only to illustrate the discursive modulations but also because it is a fairly accurate account, in its own terms, of what *is* extraordinary about Emily's speech and behaviour Similarly, the initially shocking accusation that they are after the children's money turns out to be substantially true—despite the fact that it constitutes a vicious and sexist personal attack as part of a kangaroo-court trial in the interest of mindless conformity to hierarchical Party rule. Since it demands such a complex response, the scene is not easily interpreted as a simple victimization of the Howards (whose rejoinder is a personal attack on Stephen's sister in similarly moralistic terms).

The narrative mode, then, is neither heroic nor directly comic. But if it is principally satirical at this point in the novel—its targets including both the conformists and the renegades and, in the New York scenes, their enemies both personal and political as well—it becomes more and more suffused with the agonies suffered by Emily and Stephen, whatever their motives for acting as they do. It is, Stead said, about their passion, 'passion in almost the religious sense'.[17] Like the US Communist Party itself in the postwar years, torn apart by internal dissension as well by persecution by the state, the Howards' decline and fall is attributable as much to their greed for money as it is to their conflicts of political loyalty. They have nothing to support their lavish style of living except the hope of money from 'dear Anna', Stephen's mother, and nothing to support their extravagant hopes of a better life for all except commitment to the *idea* of revolutionary change. In Paris they discover a depth of cynicism and guilt among the survivors of the war, former resistants and former collaborators alike, which profoundly shakes their American innocence. In a social context of poverty and profiteering, their attempts to establish themselves as simultaneously wealthy and good are often scarifyingly funny, yet Emily's title phrase, 'I'm dying laughing' is literally true.

The consequence of their final betrayal of Party comrades and friends is for Stephen, suicide, for Emily, madness. Yet their story could not exactly be described as a tragedy. There is something about the climactic scenes which enters the realm of farce, as Emily identifies herself finally with Stephen's capitalist family and them with Versailles, as she writes a blockbuster novel about Marie Antoinette. Her obsession with the French Revolution recalls Marx's comment in the opening lines of the *Eighteenth Brumaire*, that 'All the great events and characters in world history occur twice—the first time as tragedy, the second time as farce.'[18] It is Stead's most passionately ironic comment on the terrible history of her times, on the coexistence of tragedy and farce. The epigraphs she chose succinctly indicate the fatal mixture of modes in twentieth-century history: Part 1 has simply Gargantua's birth-cry, 'I'm thirsty!' (*Gargantua*, Rabelais), while Part 2 evokes the heroic age with: 'Renounce, renounce, on every side I hear', from Goethe's *Faust*.

The epigraph for the novel as a whole is from Walt Whitman's 'To You':

'The mockeries are not you...
The pert apparel, the deform'd attitude, drunkenness,
greed, premature death, all these I part aside...

Through angers, losses, ambition, ignorance, ennui,
what you are picks its way.'

This returns us to Stead's 'psychological drama of the person'. And it is Emily, with all these characteristics in abundance, who moves the novel along by her monstrous energy, like Nellie Cotter carried beyond caricature by the force of her passion. She is capable even at the end of turning their failure into a triumph of monstrosity:

> 'Can we too perhaps enter the annals of the red register as gorgeous monsters, human, all-too-human, a bit of Lucullus and Petronius, a bit like the Medici or even just like poor Cicero, adoring the fine life; but still faithful in our hearts...?' (p.395)

All the models for this are male, yet it is a woman's role in the novel. As a reversal of the classic situation of the nineteenth-century heroine who seeks equality in love but has no means of financial independence, Emily's fate might be read as a grim comment on emancipation. She is proud of her capacity to make big money by hard work, and speaks of it sometimes as a kind of dowry she brings to Stephen, sometimes as a kind of price she pays for his love. Small-town girl makes good? Emily has moments of cynicism ('And I'm a success! What would you call a failure?', p.153). She is perhaps the first modern Superwoman in fiction: 'I think it's possible for a woman to be a wife and mother and woman and artist and success and social worker and anything else you please in 1945' (p.81).

At the same time, Emily's distress is constantly played out in her body, the hysteric's inscription of resistance. She suffers from insomnia and countless illnesses; she overeats until she can only wear dressing-gowns; drink and drugs help to push her over the edge into madness. Although all Stead's major characters share the same compulsive restlessness, it is the women who enact it in their bodies in the manner classically designated 'hysterical'. Juliet Mitchell sees hysteria as 'the woman's simultaneous acceptance and refusal of the organisation of sexuality' in patriarchy, 'the woman's masculine language talking about feminine experience'.[19] Emily's bodily excesses closely match the excesses of her utterance—speech, writing, and laughter as well. The link is actually explicit when, rehearsing a painful story she might write about herself as a fat girl, she collapses into hysterical laughter that feels like dying:

> 'It's an awful rolling spasm, you're out of control, but madly happy, inhumanly happy, you feel as if you'll go over the edge of the precipice in another minute, and at the same time delicious, strange, only you. You feel as if now you've escaped, it's you and you're dying because it's you? (p.305)

Emily goes on to declare that she has had no such ecstatic experiences with sex, although 'nothing in my life compares with my physical feelings'. Like Stead's other 'modern women', she is sharply aware of various physical states—the associated sensations of death and ecstasy represented here recall Eleanor's experience in the opera scene of *Miss Herbert*—and expresses disappointment that 'I madly wanted to love but I wanted it to be like that. But it can't be.'

Sex may be power (as with her seduction of her stepson, Christy) or the excitement of a flirtation, or the kind of companionship she praises with Stephen, but it is never quite what she wants. She maintains that men are frightened by her, they prefer tame women (p.407). Her only experience of the 'joy' that she longed for is given by drugs, whereas 'I opened my arms to life always and received what—wooden dolls! The big empty parcels a practical joker gives you for your birthday . . .' (pp.407-8). The image suggests simultaneously the maternal aspect of her desire, and her sense of being cheated by the offer of phallic puppets for love, or 'bits of dirty paper with the halves of words written on them', the scraps of knowledge used to stuff life's trick parcel. As the most 'successful' of Stead's modern women, Emily is just as compelled as Nellie or Letty by a raging disappointment that encompasses love, knowledge, politics.

Her compensation, she maintains, is the 'monster' book, *Trial and Execution*, which is to be 'a prose epic, like Tolstoy': 'It's not only about Marie Antoinette, that's for the Midwestern mammas; it's about the flood of time and how they were carried along on it' (p.408). It is an interesting compensation, for she romanticizes the Tolstoyan determinism of the masculine epic ('man is a pawn of immense forces') while denigrating the preferences of the 'Midwestern mammas' for a detailed focus on a single life. And which kind of book is Stead writing here? Both, surely? In her political novels the women protagonists act out the confusions of political commitment and daily life, refusing to keep them separate—they force the connections, no matter how politically unsound or how personally destructive the consequences.

Monstrous Passions

It is because of this female focus, their 'different angle of seeing',[20] that Stead's political novels are so iconoclastic in relation to the genre. Two critics, both in sympathy with her political orientation, both familiar with the period about which she wrote, have commented similarly on the lack of fit in her novels between the talk and the political issues evoked. I suggest that in both instances it is a female 'angle of seeing' that might account for what Yglesias noted as Stead's success in recreating the 'full ambiance of its opportunism, charlatanism and demoralisation' from the 'fringes' of the British Left, in a narrative where *the talk is large, the concerns are petty*' (emphasis added);[21] and what Rebecca

West praised in *For Love Alone*, as 'a glimpse of the past that only the strongest, most muscular writers can give of a time (the Spanish Civil War) where 'one remembers only the passion'—quarrels, loves, deaths, returns—for the *talk* was 'too commonplace, too vague, too much the repetition of what the speakers had recently read'.[22] What both are pointing to is an inversion, in these woman-centred political novels, of the conventional hierarchy of signification over the sheer force of language and a capacity to see the centre afresh from the margins.

Do Stead's 'disorderly women', then, represent a disruption of the social order as well as the discursive? Her allusion to Rabelais, in *I'm Dying Laughing*, brings to mind the work of Bakhtin, who explored through the association of Rabelais' fiction and the folk tradition of the carnivalesque various narrative modes of transgression and excess. Kristeva's account of this work emphasized the coexistence in the carnivalesque of 'prohibitions (representation, "monologism") and their transgression (dream, body, dialogism)'.[23] The implications of its origin in carnivalesque folklore for the linguistic structures of 'Menippean discourse' are immediately relevant to a consideration of Stead's distinctive mode of writing:

> Pathological states of the soul, such as madness, split personalities, daydreams, dreams and death, become part of the narrative. . . . According to Bakhtin, these elements have more structural than thematic significance; they destroy man's epic and tragic unity as well as his belief in identity and causality. . . . It is an all-inclusive genre, put together as a pavement of citations. It includes all genres (short stories, letters, speeches, mixtures of verse and prose). . . .
>
> Put together as an exploration of the body, dreams, and language, this writing grafts onto the topical: it is a kind of

political journalism of its time. Its discourse exteriorizes political and ideological conflicts of the moment.[24]

There have been few attempts so far in feminist literary studies to apply this kind of radical genre criticism, for writing in the comic modes of farce, the grotesque, and so on, does not yet have a firm place in constructions of a 'female tradition'.[25] Stead evokes these modes, most dramatically in the two novels discussed here, but is still enough of a realist writer to leave both sides of the 'dialogical' structure firmly in place. The social order is rocked but never overturned by revolutionary possibilities; the disorderly women are all finally enclosed by the narrative, in death, madness, or just the retreat into ordinariness. Yet if they are furies, it is worth remembering that the Furies were after all political creatures, avenging the flouting of their law, their regime of power. They are quieted but not vanquished by a masculine Olympus. And so for Stead's modern women, the force of their passions constantly spills out of the 'difficult social web' spun to contain them.

Notes

Preface

1. At the time of writing there were several biographies in preparation.
2. Joan Lidoff, *Christina Stead* (New York: Ungar, 1982), p.1.
3. Four of us have subsequently published studies of her work: Joan Lidoff (ibid.), Diana Brydon and Judith Kegan Gardiner (see below) and myself.
4. She bequeathed her papers to the Australian National Library in Canberra.
5. R. G. Geering, 'What is normal? Two recent novels by Christina Stead', *Southerly*, vol.38, no.4 (1978), pp. 462–73, p.469; Laurie Clancy, *Christina Stead's 'The Man Who Loved Children' and 'For Love Alone'* (Melbourne: Shillington House, 1981), p.42; Rodney Pybus, *'Cotters' England*: In appreciation', *Stand*, vol.23, no.4 (1982), pp.40–7, p.42.
6. A European male critic warns of the danger of feminists or Australian nationalists interpreting her novels too narrowly: Rudolf Bader, 'Christina Stead and the *Bildungsroman*', *World Literature Written in English*, vol. 23, no. 1 (1984), pp. 31—9, p. 38.

Chapter 1

1. Anne Whitehead, 'Christina Stead: An Interview', *Australian Literary Studies*, vol. 6, no. 3 (1974), pp. 230–48, p. 247. Quotations in the rest of the paragraph are from this interview.
2. Rodney Wetherell, 'Interview with Christina Stead', *Australian Literary Studies*, vol. 9, no. 4 (1980), pp. 431–48, p. 439; personal communication, March 1980.
3. Whitehead, pp. 239–40.
4. Christina Stead, Papers. Manuscript Collection, Australian National Library: Ms 4967. Box 4, folder 24.
5. Ibid., Box 7, folder 53.
6. Daphne Gollan, 'The Memoirs of Cleopatra Sweatfigure', in *Women, Class and History*, ed. Elizabeth Windschuttle (Melbourne: Fontana/Collins, 1980), p. 326.
7. Doris Lessing, *The Golden Notebook* (London: Panther, 1972), p. 8.
8. Christina Stead, a letter quoted by R.G. Geering, 'Afterword', in *Ocean of Story*, ed. R.G. Geering (Ringwood, Victoria: Viking/Penguin, 1985), p. 547.
9. Christina Stead, 'On the Women's Movement', *Partisan Review*, vol. 46, no. 2 (1979), pp. 271–4, p. 274.
10. Christina Stead, *For Love Alone* (Sydney: Angus & Robertson, 1966), p. 494.
11. Christina Stead, 'The Magic Woman and Other Stories', in *Ocean of Story*, ed. R.G. Geering (Ringwood, Victoria: Viking/Penguin, 1985), p. 529.
12. Genevieve Lloyd, *The Man of Reason* (London: Methuen, 1984), pp. 81–3.
13. Virginia Woolf, 'George Eliot', in *Collected Essays* vol. 1 (London: Hogarth, 1966), p. 204.
14. Christina Stead, *For Love Alone*, pp. 495, 498.
15. Christina Stead, 'On the Women's Movement', pp. 272–3. *Partisan Review* had recently printed feminist statements by Adrienne Rich and by Susan Sontag.
16. Christina Stead, *The Man Who Loved Children* (Harmondsworth: Penguin, 1970), p. 275.
17. Christina Stead, 'The Magic Woman', pp. 529–30.
18. Ibid.
19. Simone de Beauvoir, *The Second Sex*, trans. H.M. Parshley (Harmondsworth: Penguin, 1972), passim.

20. An accessible version of this critique is found in Toril Moi, *Sexual/Textual Politics* (London: Methuen, 1985), pp. 1–18.
21. Roland Barthes, 'From Work to Text', in *Image–Music–Text*, trans. Stephen Heath (London: Fontana/Collins, 1977), p. 163.
22. Susan Sheridan, 'Feminist Readings: The Case of Christina Stead', in *Crossing Boundaries*, ed. Barbara Caine et al. (Sydney: Allen & Unwin, 1988).
23. See Mary Jacobus, *Reading Woman* (New York: Columbia University Press, 1986), especially pp. 291–4.
24. Angela Carter, 'Unhappy Families', *London Review of Books*, 16 September–6 October 1982, pp. 11–13, p. 12.
25. See Susan Higgins [Sheridan], 'For Love Alone: A Female Odyssey?', *Southerly*, vol. 38, no. 4 (1978), pp. 428–45.
26. Christina Stead, letter to Thistle Stead reproduced in Anita Segerberg, 'A Christina Stead Letter', *Australian Literary Studies*, vol. 13, no. 2 (1987), pp. 198–201, p. 199.
27. Christina Stead, Papers. Box 2, folder 7.
28. Christina Stead, *For Love Alone*, pp. 13–15.
29. Peter Brooks, *The Melodramatic Imagination* (New Haven and London: Yale University Press, 1976), p. 4.
30. 'Unhappy Families', p. 12.
31. Wetherell interview, p. 441.
32. Jonah Raskin, 'Christina Stead in Washington Square', *London Magazine*, vol. 9, no. 11 (1970), pp. 70–7, p. 75.
33. Christina Stead, *Letty Fox: Her Luck* (London: Virago, 1978), p. 458.
34. Raskin interview, p. 72.
35. Wetherell interview, p. 439.
36. Joan Lidoff, 'Christina Stead: An Interview', *Aphra*, vol. 6, nos. 3 & 4 (1976); repr. in her *Christina Stead* (New York: Ungar, 1982), p. 217.
37. Lidoff interview, p. 200; on her early training in the psychology of personality, see Anita Segerberg, 'Towards a Style of her Own', unpublished MA thesis, Auckland University, 1986.
38. Anne Chisolm, 'Stead', *National Times*, 29 March–4 April 1981, pp. 32–3.
39. Dorothy Green, 'Chaos, or a Dancing Star? Christina Stead's *Seven Poor Men of Sydney*', *Meanjin*, vol. 27, no. 2 (1968), pp. 150–61, p. 151.
40. Lidoff, *Christina Stead*, p. 13.
41. Michel Foucault, *The History of Sexuality*, vol. 1, trans. R.

Hurley (Harmondsworth: Penguin, 1981), pp. 61, 58.
42. Dugald Williamson, *Authorship and Criticism* (Sydney: Local Consumption Publications, n.d.), passim.
43. Cf. Lidoff's concept of the 'enabling myth', *Christina Stead*, pp. 17–18.
44. Roland Barthes, 'The Death of the Author', in *Image-Music-Text*, p.143.
45. Williamson, *Authorship and Criticism*, pp. 22–3.
46. Michel Foucault, 'What Is an Author?', trans. J.V. Harari, in *Textual Strategies*, ed. J.V. Harari (London: Methuen, 1979), pp. 141–60. This formulation is from Meaghan Morris, 'Apologia (*Beyond Deconstruction*/"Beyond What?")', *Scripsi*, vol. 4, no. 4 (1987), pp. 133–46, pp. 136–7.
47. 'The Death of the Author', p.143.
48. Nancy K. Miller, 'Changing the Subject: Authorship, Writing and Gender', in *Feminist Studies/Critical Studies*, ed. Teresa de Lauretis (Bloomington: Indiana University Press, 1986), pp. 102–20, p. 104.
49. Williamson, *Authorship and Criticism*, p. 1.
50. Christina Stead, 'A Writer's Friends' in *Ocean of Story*, pp. 494–502, p. 497.
51. Virginia Woolf, *A Room of One's Own* [1928] (Harmondsworth: Penguin, 1972), p. 89.
52. Christina Stead, Papers. Box 1, folder 1.
53. Teresa de Lauretis, 'Feminist Studies/Critical Studies: Issues, Terms and Contexts', in *Feminist Studies/Critical Studies*, pp. 1–19, p. 9.

Chapter 2

1. Angela Carter, 'Unhappy Families', p. 11.
2. Randall Jarrell, 'An Unread Book', in Christina Stead, *The Man Who Loved Children* (Harmondsworth: Penguin, 1970), p. 1. Further references to this edition in text.
3. Engels, *The Origin of the Family, Private Property and the State*, cited by Terry Sturm, 'Christina Stead's New Realism', in *Cunning Exiles*, eds. D. Anderson and S. Knight (Sydney: Angus & Robertson, 1974), pp. 9–35, p. 20.
4. Susan Sheridan, '*The Man Who Loved Children* and the Patriarchal Family Drama', in *Gender, Politics and Fiction*, ed. Carole Ferrier (St Lucia: University of Queensland Press, 1985), pp. 136–49.
5. See Christina Stead, 'A Waker and a Dreamer', in *Ocean of*

Story, pp. 490–1.

6. On some connections between Roosevelt, eugenics and social improvement, see Donna Haraway, 'Teddy Bear Patriarchy: Taxidermy in the Garden of Eden, New York City, 1908–36', *Social Text*, no. 11 (Winter 1984–5), pp. 20–64.

7. Jose Yglesias, 'Marx as Muse', *Nation* (New York) (5 April 1965), pp. 363–70, p. 369.

8. Jonathan Arac, 'The Struggle for Cultural Heritage: Christina Stead Refunctions Charles Dickens and Mark Twain', *Cultural Critique*, no. 2 (1986), p. 171–89, p. 180; Arac also points out that Sam's surname is that of Harry Pollitt, a founding member of the British Communist Party who became a national figure during the Popular Front period of the late 1930s.

9. Jennifer McDonell, 'Christina Stead's *The Man Who Loved Children*', *Southerly*, vol. 44, no. 4 (1984), pp. 394–413, p. 401.

10. Randall Jarrell, 'An Unread Book', p. 11.

11. Ibid., p. 31.

12. On Stead's uses of Nietzsche in this novel, see Shirley Walker, 'Language, Art and Ideas in *The Man Who Loved Children*', *Meridian*, vol. 2, no. 1 (1983), pp. 11–20; Rebecca Baker, 'Christina Stead: the Nietzsche Connection' and Ken Stewart, 'Heaven and Hell in *The Man Who Loved Children*', *Meridian*, vol. 2, no. 2 (1983), pp. 116–20 and pp. 121–7, respectively.

13. Dorothy Green, '*The Man Who Loved Children*: Storm in a Teacup', in *The Australian Experience*, ed. W.S. Ramson (Canberra: ANU Press, 1974), pp. 174–208, p. 176.

14. Ibid., p. 207.

15. Joan Lidoff, *Christina Stead*, pp. 37–8.

16. Ibid., p. 53.

17. On the assumption that women's texts will express their author's 'female rage' see Toril Moi, *Sexual/Textual Politics*, p. 62.

18. Judith Kegan Gardiner, 'A Wake for Mother', *Feminist Studies*, 4, June 1978, pp. 145–65, p. 147.

19. Judith Kegan Gardiner, 'The Heroine as her Author's Daughter', in *Feminist Criticism*, eds. Cheryl Brown and Karen Olsen (Metuchen, NJ: Scarecrow Press, 1978), pp. 244–53, p. 251.

20. Identified as the book's feminist element in Pauline

Nestor, 'An Impulse to Self-Expression: *The Man Who Loved Children'*, *Critical Review*, no. 18 (1976), pp. 61–78, p. 72.

21. Diana Brydon, *Christina Stead* (London: Macmillan, 1987) states, mistakenly in my view, that the novel marks a turning towards female support systems (p. 78).

22. Judith Kegan Gardiner, 'On Female Identity and Writing by Women', *Critical Inquiry*, vol. 8, no. 2 (1981), pp. 347–61, p. 361; this number repr. as *Writing and Sexual Difference*, ed. Elizabeth Abel (Chicago: University of Chicago Press, 1982).

23. Ibid., p. 352. Gardiner later criticizes the mother-daughter theory in that it 'separates empathy from history': 'Gender, Values and Lessing's Cats', in *Feminist Issues in Literary Scholarship*, ed. Shari Benstock (Bloomington: Indiana University Press, 1987), pp. 110—23, p. 117.

24. Teresa de Lauretis, *Alice Doesn't: Feminism, Semiotics and Cinema* (Bloomington: Indiana University Press, 1984), p. 142.

25. Ibid., p. 143.

26. Judith Kegan Gardiner, 'On Female Identity', p. 358.

27. Susan Sheridan, 'The Patriarchal Family Drama'.

28. Sandra Gilbert, 'Life's Empty Pack: Notes toward a Literary Daughteronomy', *Critical Inquiry*, vol. 11 (March 1985), pp. 355–84, mentions this novel as an example of the father–daughter incest story or fable but does not regard its ending as utopian, seeing Louie rather as 'a murderess and an outlaw' (p. 376).

29. Percy Bysshe Shelley, 'The Cenci', in *Poetical Works*, ed. Thomas Hutchinson (London: Oxford University Press, 1961), pp. 274–337.

30. Luce Irigaray, *Speculum of the Other Woman*, trans. Gillian Gill (Ithaca, NY: Cornell University Press, 1985), p. 133.

31. Jane Gallop, *Feminism and Psychoanalysis: the Daughter's Seduction* (London: Methuen, 1982), pp. 70–1.

32. For example *In Dora's Case*, eds. Charles Bernheimer and Claire Kahane (London: Virago, 1985); Hélène Cixous and Catherine Clément, *The Newly Born Woman*, trans. Betsy Wing (Minneapolis: University of Minnesota Press, 1986).

33. Luce Irigaray, *Speculum*, p. 38; emphasis in original.

34. Jane Gallop, *Feminism and Psychoanalysis*, p. 71.

35. Ibid., p. 76.

36. Julia Kristeva, *Revolution in Poetic Language*, trans. Margaret Waller (New York: Columbia University Press, 1984), pp. 21–30 and passim.
37. Toril Moi, *Sexual/Textual Politics*, p. 161.
38. Barry Hill, 'Christina Stead at 80 Says Love is her Religion', *Sydney Morning Herald*, Saturday, 17 July, 1982, p. 33; she is reported here as insisting that she used to know *Thus Spake Zarathustra* by heart, for the poetry but not for the philosophy.

Chapter 3

1. Christina Stead, *For Love Alone* (Sydney: Angus & Robertson, 1969), p. 14. Further references to this edition in text.
2. Lorna Sage, 'Inheriting the Future: *For Love Alone*', *Stand*, vol. 23, no. 4 (1982), pp. 34–9, p. 35.
3. Christina Stead, Papers. Box 1, folder 2; see also her 'Another View of the Homestead', in *Ocean of Story*, pp. 513–20, p. 517.
4. Wetherell interview, p. 439.
5. For an early example, see Jean Saxelby and Gwen Walker-Smith, 'Christina Stead', *Biblionews* vol. 2, no. 9 (1949), pp. 37–43.
6. See, for example Brian Kiernan, 'Christina Stead: *Seven Poor Men of Sydney* and *For Love Alone*', in *Images of Society and Nature* (Melbourne: Oxford University Press, 1971), pp. 59–81; Ian Reid, ' "The Woman Problem" in Some Australian and New Zealand Novels', *Southern Review* (Adelaide), vol. 7, no. 3 (1974), pp. 187–204.
7. Putnam's translation of *Don Quixote*, quoted by R. G. Geering, *Christina Stead* (Sydney: Angus & Robertson, 1979), p. 119.
8. See Drusilla Modjeska, *Exiles at Home: Australian Women Writers, 1925–1945* (Sydney: Angus & Robertson, 1981), pp. 20–5.
9. These are more fully documented in Ian Reid, ' "The Woman Problem". . . .'.
10. Michael Wilding, 'Christina Stead's Australian Novels', *Southerly*, vol. 27, no.1 (1967), pp. 20–23, p. 28.
11. I refer to the account of Bakhtin by Julia Kristeva,

Desire in Language, trans. Leon S. Roudiez *et al.* (Oxford: Basil Blackwell, 1980), pp. 64–72.

12. R. J. Schofield, 'The Man Who Loved Christina Stead', *Bulletin*, May 22 (1965), pp. 29–31, p. 31.
13. Ian Reid, ' "The Woman Problem". . .', pp. 108–10.
14. Tony Davies, 'Transports of Delight: Fiction and its Audiences in the Later Nineteenth Century', in *Formations of Pleasure*, ed. Formations Collective (London: Routledge & Kegan Paul, 1983), pp. 46–58, p. 56.
15. Elizabeth Abel, Marianne Hirsch and Elizabeth Langland (eds), *The Voyage In: Fictions of Female Development* (Hanover and London: New England University Press, 1983), Introduction, pp. 11–12.
16. Ibid., pp. 12–13.
17. Ibid., p. 13.
18. Ibid., p. 10, quoting from *The Reproduction of Mothering* (Berkeley: University of California Press, 1978), p. 169.
19. Ibid., p. 10, referring to Gilligan's *In a Different Voice: Psychological Theory and Women's Development* (Cambridge, Mass.: Harvard University Press, 1982).
20. Susan Gubar, 'The Birth of the Artist as Heroine', in *The Representation of Women in Fiction*, ed. Carolyn Heilbrun and Margaret Higonnet (Baltimore and London: Johns Hopkins University Press, 1983), pp. 19–59, p. 39.
21. Ibid., p. 50.
22. Rachel Blau DuPlessis, *Writing Beyond the Ending* (Bloomington: Indiana University Press, 1985), p. 91.
23. Ibid., p. 94.
24. Ibid., p. 99.
25. Ibid., p. 103.
26. Diana Brydon, *Christina Stead*, p. 82; Joan Lidoff, *Christina Stead*, p. 58.
27. M. M. Bakhtin, *Speech Genres and Other Late Essays*, trans. Vern McGee (Austin: University of Texas Press, 1986), pp. 23–4.
28. George Eliot, *Middlemarch* (London: Oxford University Press, 1947), pp. xv–xvi.
29. Nancy Miller, discussing this theme in *Villette*, comments on 'the way in which female desire as quest aligns itself uneasily with the question of mastery. . . , mastery and knowledge within an academy': 'Changing the Subject', p. 112.

30. This comparison with *Middlemarch* was developed in my earlier essay: Susan Higgins, *'For Love Alone*: A Female Odyssey?', pp. 441–3.
31. R. G. Geering, *Christina Stead*, p. 112.
32. Joan Lidoff, *Christina Stead*, pp. 59–60.
33. Jennifer Strauss, 'An Unsentimental Romance', *Kunapipi*, vol. 4, no. 2 (1982), pp. 82–94, p. 92.

Chapter 4

1. Christina Stead, *Letty Fox: Her Luck* (London: Virago, 1978), p. 502. Further references to this edition in the text.
2. Christina Stead, *Miss Herbert (The Suburban Wife)* (New York: Random House, 1976), p. 308. Further references to this edition in the text.
3. Elaine Showalter, 'Towards a Feminist Poetics', in *Women Writing and Writing About Women*, ed. Mary Jacobus (London: Croom Helm, 1979), pp. 22–41, p. 27.
4. Christina Stead, referring to Eleanor Herbert, personal communication, 28.12.1975.
5. Pamela Law, 'Letty Fox, Her Luck', *Southerly*, vol. 38, no. 4 (1978), pp. 448–53, pp. 449, 452.
6. Angela Carter, 'Unhappy Families', p. 12.
7. The Conservative Party's history of wooing women voters with 'feminine' adaptations of this ideology is discussed by Beatrix Campbell, *Iron Ladies: Why Do Women Vote Tory?* (London: Virago, 1987).
8. Christina Stead, Papers. Box 3, folder 18.
9. Helen Yglesias, 'Christina Stead, Australia's Neglected Maverick', *National Times*, 5–10 July 1976, p. 19.
10. Christina Stead, *Cotters' England* (London: Secker & Warburg, 1967), p. 294.
11. Mary Kathleen Benet, 'Introduction', *Letty Fox* (Virago) n.p.
12. Christina Stead, Papers. Box 2, folder 7.
13. Elizabeth Perkins, 'Energy and Originality in Some Characters of Christina Stead', *Journal Of Commonwealth Literature*, vol. 15, no. 1 (1980), pp. 107–13, p. 109.
14. R. G. Geering, *Christina Stead*, p. 131.
15. Angela Carter, 'Unhappy Families', p. 12.

16. Diana Brydon, *Christina Stead*, p. 100.
17. Meaghan Morris, 'Introduction', *Letty Fox* (Sydney: Angus & Robertson, 1974) n.p.
18. A similar problem is encountered in reading Stead's male portrait of the same period, *A Little Tea, A Little Chat* (1948).
19. Elizabeth Perkins, 'Energy and Originality. . .', p. 113.
20. Diana Brydon, *Christina Stead*, pp. 151–6.
21. Christina Stead, *The Beauties and Furies* (London: Virago, 1982), p. 150.
22. Christina Stead, *For Love Alone*, pp. 489–90.
23. Susan Sheridan, 'Feminist Readings. . .'.
24. Stead's papers contain a synopsis of the novel in these terms, apparently directed to an Eastern bloc readership, emphasizing the pretensions to gentility of this group of workers, which makes them so susceptible to economic and, by implication, intellectual exploitation: Christina Stead, Papers. Box 3, folder 18.

Chapter 5

1. Christina Stead, *Cotters' England* (London: Secker & Warburg, 1967); Christina Stead, *I'm Dying Laughing: The Humourist* (London: Virago, 1986). Further references to these editions in the text.
2. Whitehead interview, p. 246.
3. Cf. 'King Arthur in his mound, gods and Herne the Hunter in the woods, green folk, little folk, squirrel-faced elves. . . . And all this is in the people, in their unconscious thoughts and their language': Christina Stead, 'Another View of the Homestead', p. 518.
4. For example, R. G. Geering, *Christina Stead*, pp. 155–60.
5. For example, Louise Adler, 'Retreat into two-fold gluttony', *Times on Sunday*, 19 April 1987, p. 30; but another stresses the personal at the expense of taking the politics seriously: Adrian Mitchell, 'Accessible and still in good Stead', *Weekend Australian Magazine*, 28–29 March 1987, p. 15.
6. Terry Sturm, 'Christina Stead's New Realism', p. 25.
7. Ibid., p. 21.
8. As Louie refers to herself in *The Man Who Loved Children*, p. 349.

9. The 'Jago' was a notorious criminal slum of late Victorian London, and the subject of Arthur Morrison's fiction, *The Child of the Jago* (1896): Raphael Samuel, Preface, *East End Underworld,* ed. Raphael Samuel (London: Routledge & Kegan Paul, 1981). I am grateful to Susan Magarey for this reference.
10. Jose Yglesias, 'Marking off a chunk of England', *Nation* (New York), 24 October 1966, pp. 420-1, p. 421.
11. Diana Brydon, *Christina Stead,* p. 128.
12. Louis Althusser, *Lenin and Philosophy and Other Essays,* trans. Ben Brewster (London: New Left Books, 1971), pp. 153–5.
13. Gayatri Spivak, 'The Politics of Interpretations', *Critical Inquiry,* vol. 9 (1982), pp. 259–78, p. 264.
14. Whitehead interview, p. 246, quoted in Geering's Preface to the novel.
15. See her report: Christina Stead, 'The Writers Take Sides', *Left Review,* vol. 1, no. 2 (1935), pp. 453–63 and 469–75.
16. On this and other matters, including Party attitudes to women's issues, see Peggy Dennis, *The Autobiography of an American Communist* (Westport/Berkeley: Lawrence Hill, 1977).
17. Quoted in Geering's Preface to the novel.
18. Karl Marx, 'The Eighteenth Brumaire of Louis Bonaparte', in *The Marx and Engels Reader,* ed. Robert Tucker (New York: Norton, 1972), pp. 436–525, p. 436.
19. Juliet Mitchell, 'Femininity, Narrative and Psychoanalysis', in *The Longest Revolution* (London: Virago, 1984), pp. 287–94, p. 288-9.
20. Christina Stead, 'The Magic Woman. . .', p. 530.
21. Jose Yglesias, 'Marking off a Chunk of England', p. 421.
22. Rebecca West, 'Christina Stead: a Tribute', *Stand,* vol. 23, no. 4 (1982), pp. 31–3, p. 33.
23. Julia Kristeva, *Desire in Language,* p. 78.
24. Ibid., p. 83.
25. But see, for example, Sneja Gunew, 'Rosa Cappiello's *Oh Lucky Country*: Multicultural Reading Strategies', *Meanjin,* vol. 44, no. 4 (1985), pp. 517–28.

Select Bibliography

A bibliography: Marianne Ehrhardt, 'Christina Stead: a Checklist', *Australian Literary Studies*, vol. 9, no. 4, (1980), pp. 508–35.
Christina Stead, Papers. Manuscript Collection, Australian National Library: Ms 4967.

Major Works by Christina Stead

Books
(The details refer to first publications; editions used in this study are given in the endnotes.)
The Salzburg Tales (London: Peter Davies, 1934; New York: D. Appleton-Century, 1934).
Seven Poor Men of Sydney (London: Peter Davies, 1934; New York: D. Appleton-Century, 1935).
The Beauties and Furies (London: Peter Davies, 1936; New York: D. Appleton-Century, 1936).
House Of All Nations (New York: Simon & Schuster, 1938; London: Peter Davies, 1938).
The Man Who Loved Children (New York: Simon & Schuster, 1940; London: Peter Davies, 1941).
For Love Alone (New York: Harcourt Brace, 1944; Peter Davies, 1945).
Letty Fox: Her Luck (New York: Harcourt Brace, 1946; London: Peter Davies, 1947).

A Little Tea, A Little Chat (New York: Harcourt Brace, 1948).

The People With the Dogs (Boston: Little Brown, 1952).

[*Dark Places of the Heart*] (New York: Holt, Rhinehart & Winston, 1966). Pub. in London as: *Cotters' England* (London: Secker & Warburg, 1967).

The Puzzleheaded Girl (New York: Holt, Rhinehart & Winston, 1967; London: Secker & Warburg, 1968).

The Little Hotel (Sydney: Angus & Robertson, 1973; New York: Holt, Rhinehart & Winston, 1975).

Miss Herbert (The Suburban Wife) (New York: Random House, 1976).

Posthumous publications

Ocean of Story, The uncollected stories of Christina Stead, edited with an afterword by R. G. Geering (Ringwood, Victoria: Viking/Penguin, 1985).

I'm Dying Laughing: The Humourist, edited with a preface by R. G. Geering (London: Virago, 1986).

The Palace with Several Sides: A Sort of Love Story, limited edition, edited by R. G. Geering (Canberra: Officina Brindabella, 1986); repr. in *Southerly*, vol. 47, no. 2 (1987), pp. 115–25.

Collections

Modern Women in Love: Sixty Twentieth-Century Masterpieces of Fiction, edited by Christina Stead and William Blake (New York: Dryden Press, 1945).

Essays

Stead, Christina, 'The Writers Take Sides', *Left Review*, vol. 1, no. 2 (1935), pp. 453–63 and 469–75.

Stead, Christina, 'On the Women's Movement', *Partisan Review*, vol. 46, no. 2(1979), pp. 271–4.

Interviews (A Selection)

Beston, John, 'An Interview with Christina Stead', *World Literature Written in English*, vol. 15, no. 1 (1976), pp. 87–95.

Guiffre, Guilia, 'Christina Stead', *Stand*, vol. 23, no. 4 (1982), pp. 22–9.

Lidoff, Joan, 'Christina Stead: An Interview', *Aphra*, vol. 6, nos. 3 & 4 (1976), pp. 39–64; repr. in her *Christina Stead* (New York: Ungar, 1982).

Raskin, Jonah, 'Christina Stead in Washington Square', *London Magazine*, vol. 9, no. 11 (1970), pp. 70–7.

Wetherell, Rodney, 'Interview with Christina Stead', *Australian Literary Studies*, vol. 9, no. 4 (1980), pp. 431–48.

Whitehead, Anne, 'Christina Stead: An Interview', *Australian Literary Studies*, vol. 6, no. 3 (1974), pp. 230–48.

Critical Works on Christina Stead

Books

Brydon, Diana, *Christina Stead* (London:Macmillan, 1987).

Clancy, Laurie, *Christina Stead's 'The Man Who Loved Children' and 'For Love Alone'* (Melbourne: Shillington House, 1981).

Geering, R. G., *Christina Stead* (New York: Twayne, 1969; rev. edn, Sydney: Angus & Robertson, 1979).

Lidoff, Joan, *Christina Stead* (New York: Ungar, 1982).

Articles, Essays and Reviews

Adler, Louise, 'Retreat into Two-fold Gluttony', *Times on Sunday*, 19 April 1987, p. 30.

Arac, Jonathan, 'The Struggle for Cultural Heritage: Christina Stead Refunctions Charles Dickens and Mark Twain', *Cultural Critique*, no. 2 (1986), p. 171–89.

Bader, Rudolf, 'Christina Stead and the *Bildungsroman*', *World Literature Written in English*, vol. 23, no. 1 (1984), pp. 31–9.

Baker, Rebecca, 'Christina Stead: the Nietzsche Connection', *Meridian*, vol. 2, no. 2 (1983), pp. 116–20.

Carter, Angela, 'Unhappy Families', *London Review of Books*, 16 September–6 October 1982, pp. 11–13.

Chisholm, Anne, 'Stead', *National Times*, 29 March—4 April, 1981, pp. 32—3.

Geering R. G., 'What is normal? Two recent novels by Christina Stead', *Southerly*, vol. 38, no. 4 (1978), pp. 462—73.

Green, Dorothy, '*The Man Who Loved Children*: Storm in a Teacup', in *The Australian Experience*, ed. W. S. Ramson (Canberra: ANU Press, 1974), pp. 174–208.

Green, Dorothy, 'Chaos, or a Dancing Star? Christina Stead's *Seven Poor Men of Sydney*', *Meanjin*, vol. 27, no. 2 (1968), pp. 150—61.

Higgins [Sheridan], Susan, '*For Love Alone*: A Female Odyssey?', *Southerly*, vol. 38, no. 4 (1978), pp. 428—45.

Kiernan, Brian, 'Christina Stead: *Seven Poor Men of Sydney* and *For Love Alone*', in *Images of Society and Nature* (Melbourne: Oxford University Press, 1971), pp. 59–81.

Law, Pamela, 'Letty Fox, Her Luck', *Southerly*, vol. 38, no. 4 (1978), pp. 448–53.

McDonell, Jennifer, 'Christina Stead's *The Man Who Loved Children*', *Southerly*, vol. 44, no. 4 (1984), pp. 394–413.

Mitchell, Adrian, 'Accessible and Still in Good Stead', *Weekend Australian Magazine*, 28–9 March 1987, p. 15.

Nestor, Pauline, 'An Impulse to Self-Expression: *The Man Who Loved Children*', *Critical Review*, no. 18 (1976), pp. 61–78.

Perkins, Elizabeth, 'Energy and Originality in Some Characters of Christina Stead', *Journal of Commonwealth Literature*, vol. 15, no. 1 (1980), pp. 107—13.

Pybus, Rodney, '*Cotters' England*: In appreciation', *Stand*, vol. 23, no. 4 (1982), pp. 40–7.

Reid, Ian, ' "The Woman Problem" in Some Australian and New Zealand Novels', *Southern Review* (Adelaide), vol. 7, no. 3 (1974), pp. 187–204.

Sage, Lorna, 'Inheriting the Future: *For Love Alone*', *Stand*, vol. 23, no. 4 (1982), pp. 34–9.

Saxelby, Jean and Gwen Walker-Smith, 'Christina Stead', *Biblionews*, vol. 2, no. 9 (1949), pp. 37—43.

Schofield, R. J., 'The Man Who Loved Christina Stead',

Select Bibliography

Bulletin, May 22 (1965), pp. 29-31.

Segerberg, Anita, 'A Christina Stead Letter', *Australian Literary Studies*, vol. 13, no. 2 (1987), pp. 198-201.

Segerberg, Anita, 'Towards a Style of her Own', unpublished MA thesis, Auckland University, 1986.

Sheridan, Susan, 'Feminist Readings. The Case of Christina Stead', in *Crossing Boundaries*, ed. Barbara Caine et al. (Sydney: Allen & Unwin, forthcoming 1988).

Sheridan, Susan, '*The Man Who Loved Children* and the Patriarchal Family Drama', in *Gender, Politics and Fiction*, ed. Carole Ferrier (St Lucia: University of Queensland Press, 1985), pp. 136-49.

Stewart, Ken, 'Heaven and Hell in *The Man Who Loved Children*', *Meridian*, vol. 2, no. 2 (1983), pp. 121-7.

Strauss, Jennifer, 'An Unsentimental Romance', *Kunapipi*, vol. 4, no. 2 (1982), pp. 82-94.

Sturm, Terry, 'Christina Stead's New Realism', in *Cunning Exiles*, eds. D. Anderson and S. Knight (Sydney: Angus & Robertson, 1974), pp. 9-35.

Walker, Shirley, 'Language, Art and Ideas in *The Man Who Loved Children*', *Meridian*, vol. 2, no. 1 (1983), pp. 11-20.

West, Rebecca, 'Christina Stead: a Tribute', *Stand*, vol. 23, no. 4 (1982), pp. 31-3.

Wilding, Michael, 'Christina Stead's Australian Novels', *Southerly*, vol. 27, no. 1 (1967), pp. 20-33.

Yglesias, Helen, 'Christina Stead, Australia's Neglected Maverick', *National Times*, 5-10 July 1976, p. 19.

Yglesias, Jose, 'Marking off a Chunk of England', *Nation* (New York), 24 October 1966, pp. 420-1.

Yglesias, Jose, 'Marx as Muse', *Nation* (New York), 5 April 1965, pp. 363-70.

Critical Theory and Background

Abel, Elizabeth (ed.), *Writing and Sexual Difference* (Chicago: University of Chicago Press, 1982).

Abel, Elizabeth, Marianne Hirsch and Elizabeth Langland (eds), *The Voyage In: Fictions of Female*

Christina Stead

Development (Hanover and London: New England University Press, 1983).

Bakhtin, M. M., *Speech Genres and Other Late Essays*, trans. Vern McGee (Austin: University of Texas Press, 1986).

Barthes, Roland, 'From Work to Text', in *Image—Music—Text*, trans. Stephen Heath (London: Fontana/Collins, 1977).

Beauvoir, Simone de, *The Second Sex*, trans. H. M. Parshley (Harmondsworth: Penguin, 1972).

Brooks, Peter, *The Melodramatic Imagination* (New Haven and London: Yale University Press, 1976).

DuPlessis, Rachel Blau, *Writing Beyond the Ending* (Bloomington: Indiana University Press, 1985).

Foucault, Michel, 'What Is an Author?', trans. J. V. Harari, in *Textual Strategies*, ed. J. V. Harari (London: Methuen, 1979), pp. 141–60.

Gallop, Jane, *Feminism and Psychoanalysis: the Daughter's Seduction* (London: Methuen, 1982).

Gardiner, Judith Kegan, 'A Wake for Mother', *Feminist Studies*, 4, June 1978, pp. 145–65.

Gardiner, Judith Kegan, 'On Female Identity and Writing by Women', *Critical Inquiry*, vol. 8, no. 2 (1981), pp. 347–61.

Gardiner, Judith Kegan, 'The Heroine as her Author's Daughter', in *Feminist Criticism*, eds. Cheryl Brown and Karen Olsen (Metuchen, NJ: Scarecrow Press, 1978), pp. 244—53.

Gilbert, Sandra, 'Life's Empty Pack: Notes toward a Literary Daughteronomy', *Critical Inquiry*, vol. 11, March 1985, pp. 355–84.

Gubar, Susan, 'The Birth of the Artist as Heroine', in *The Representation of Women in Fiction*, ed. Carolyn Heilbrun and Margaret Higonnet (Baltimore and London: Johns Hopkins University Press, 1983), pp. 19–59.

Gunew, Sneja, 'Rosa Cappiello's *Oh Lucky Country*: Multicultural Reading Strategies', *Meanjin*, vol. 44, no. 4 (1985), pp. 517–28.

Irigaray, Luce, *Speculum of the Other Woman*, trans. Gillian Gill (Ithaca, NY: Cornell University Press, 1985).

Jacobus, Mary, *Reading Woman* (New York: Columbia University Press, 1986).

Kristeva, Julia, *Desire in Language*, trans. Leon S. Roudiez *et al.* (Oxford: Basil Blackwell, 1980).

Kristeva, Julia, *Revolution in Poetic Language*, trans. Margaret Waller (New York: Columbia University Press, 1984).

Lauretis, Teresa de, 'Feminist Studies/Critical Studies: Issues, Terms and Contexts', in *Feminist Studies/Critical Studies*, ed. Teresa de Lauretis (Bloomington: Indiana University Press, 1986), pp. 1–19.

Lauretis, Teresa de, *Alice Doesn't: Feminism, Semiotics and Cinema* (Bloomington: Indiana Unviersity Press, 1984).

Lloyd Genevieve, *The Man of Reason* (London: Methuen, 1984).

Miller, Nancy K., 'Changing the Subject: Authorship, Writing and Gender', in *Feminist Studies/Critical Studies*, ed. Teresa de Lauretis (Bloomington: Indiana University Press, 1986), pp. 102–20.

Mitchell, Juliet, 'Femininity, Narrative and Psychoanalysis', in *The Longest Revolution* (London: Virago, 1984), pp. 287–94.

Modjeska, Drusilla, *Exiles at Home: Australian Women Writers, 1925–1945* (Sydney: Angus & Robertson, 1981).

Moi, Toril, *Sexual/Textual Politics* (London: Methuen, 1985).

Showalter, Elaine, 'Towards a Feminist Poetics', in *Women Writing and Writing About Women*, ed. Mary Jacobus (London: Croom Helm, 1979), pp. 22–41.

Spivak, Gayatri, 'The Politics of Interpretations', *Critical Inquiry*, vol. 9 (1982), pp. 259–78.

Williamson, Dugald, *Authorship and Criticism* (Sydney: Local Consumption Publications, n.d.).

Woolf, Virginia, *A Room of One's Own* [1928] (Harmondsworth: Penguin, 1972).

Woolf, Virginia, 'George Eliot', in *Collected Essays* vol. 1 (London: Hogarth, 1966).

Index

Index

NOTTINGHAM UNIVERSITY LIBRARY